true from our first profession of faith. It is true when we start each new discipline. It is true when we become aware of the depths of our sin and mindful of our need to be continually repenting. It is true when we become willing to be completely dependent on and open with God—intimate with Him. Then we must repent of our unbelief again if we are to fully surrender to a calling.

Don't put off your decision to move closer to God and hear His voice. Get your copy of *God Called - He Needs Your Decision!* today and get started on a journey that will lead to a fully surrendered life.

Serious Disciples of Jesus should read *God Called - He Needs Your Decision!* Because, according to one reviewer:

If a baby were born and failed to thrive, the family would rightly consider it a great tragedy. When a Christian is born and fails to thrive, however, many people don't notice. *God Called—He Needs Your Decision!* by Randy Kirk is an invitation to Christians to thrive. It is a spiritual counterattack to the widespread misconception that "being" a Christian is a passive state. Randy invites Christians to "do" Christianity.

Katherine Harms, Editor

Are you ready to ratchet up your devotion to God and Jesus to the next level?
***God Called - He Needs Your Decision!* is perfect for you**

Do you sometimes feel stuck in your walk and desire to be of greater service?
***God Called* was written for Christians just like you**

Are you the first to sign up for any seminar that teaches how to find out God's will for your life?
The pathway to that answer for you is one click away.

God Called is not for the lukewarm - UNLESS you are ready to repent of being lukewarm

God Called is not for the prodigal - UNLESS you are tired of eating with the pigs

God Called is not for pew dusters - UNLESS you are prepared to step outside your comfort zone

Here's what others are saying:

Even as a Pastor sometimes we can lose focus on what it really is to be a true disciple of Christ.
I would recommend it to any Pastor or leader of a church.
Great Stuff!

   Robert Hill - Administrative Pastor
   Core Church Los Angeles

Just reading the first few pages, God spoke a quick word to me, setting me free from years of bondage to what people will think of me if I follow Jesus full out. Using Randy's simple steps of faith, this is a must-read for your next step in growing in grace.

Cheryl Colwell - Author - *The Secrets of Montebellis* and *The Proof*

The Psalmist tells us that deep calls unto deep . . . Take the plunge into the River of Life with Randy Kirk's newest book, *God Called—He Needs Your Decision!* and drink deep from the well that never runs dry. Find keys to intimacy with Father, Son, and Holy Spirit hidden in plain sight. Come away refreshed and longing for more of Him.

Michael J. Webb, Bestselling Author of *The Master's Quilt*

God Called was written specifically for mature Christians who feel they have not really heard the Lord speak to them. These Christians truly want to hear the voice of God calling to them with an offer to serve in a capacity that is outside of their expectations.

Review these questions, and one of which might be holding you back from hearing God's plan for your life:

- Jesus says disciples need to carry their cross and follow Him. Can you do that?
- Jesus said that disciples must hate mother and father (compared to Him) Is that you?
- Jesus said that disciples must obey what he has commanded. Do you?
- Jesus said that disciples must give up everything. Are you prepared to do so?
- Dallas Willard says "very few Christians want to hear what God has to say. Do you?

Here's a sample of the impactful words from *God Called* that have encouraged readers to take their Christianity to the next level:

Our Christian walk is always about how much we trust and believe, and whether we trust God enough to put aside our fear. Each stage of our maturing in Christ depends on our ability to repent of our unbelief, or pride, and our idols, and move to the next stage. This is

God Called
He Needs Your Decision!

by

Randy W. Kirk

Send Me! Press

Copyright 2014 by Randy Kirk
All rights reserved

No part of this book may be reproduced or transmitted in any form or by any means, electronic or mechanical, including photocopying, recording or by any information storage and retrieval system, without written permission from the author, except for the inclusion of brief quotations in review.

All Scripture quotations, in this publication are from the HOLY BIBLE, NEW INTERNATIONAL VERSION® NIV® Copyright © 1973, 1978, 1984, 2011 by Biblica, Inc.®. Used by permission. All rights reserved worldwide.

ISBN 978-0-9960597-1-8 (pbk.)
ISBN 978-0-9960597-0-1 (ebk.)

First edition 2014

Printed in the United States of America

Library of Congress Control Number: 2014906852

1 2 3 4 5 6 7 8 9 10

Table of Contents

Dedication ii
Acknowledgments iii
Introduction 1
1. Be a Disciple 5
Feature Story: *Follow God's Clear Call* 15
2. Go For Him 23
3. Hear His Voice 26
4. Be Intimate 29
5. Mature in Discipline 36
6. Trust Him Completely 44
7. Be Vulnerable 54
Feature Story: *Sin Gets in the Way* 70
8. Listen at All Times 74
9. Surrender 87
10. Be Holy 93
End Notes 102
Suggested Reading 103
Photo Credits 104

Dedication

God sent two angels to keep me focused during a very difficult time. That time of trouble helped give me a deeper love for and understanding of our Savior. My sister, Judy Stockwell, was a solid rock. My daughter, Christian Nichols, provided loving nurture. This book could not have been written without their care and concern through the dark time.

Acknowledgments

There are many individuals who contributed time and energy to this work. At the top of the list is my dear friend, Eric Snyder. He has given more ideas and encouragement than almost anyone else. Eric wrote the last several paragraphs of the introduction. He made me think through some places that may have been rough, but kept me going through his generous praise.

My brother, Gary Kirk, was a huge help in suggesting major additions to certain sections along with resources that would help me flesh them out. Several of these ideas turned out to be critical bridges without which some of the journey would have been much more treacherous.

The editor, Katherine Harms, was a miracle find. Her editing was as strong as any I have had from any publisher, but the ideas that flowed from her own Christian maturity were often more helpful than even the better grammar or other more mundane corrections. Thanks for all your red ink.

A group of Christian authors under the banner of John 3:16 Marketing Group provided several early stage readers who gave thoughtful direction. Thanks to Lorilyn Roberts, founder and fearless leader of the group, who offered many ideas along the way. Carole Brown gave solid direction and much needed encouragement. Lelia Rose Foreman gave some hard to swallow, but helpful direction.

For additional theological help, I was pleased to have Robert Hill, the assistant pastor of Core Church, Los Angeles, give the book a long, hard look. Other friends and family, and especially Nathan Nichols and Dory Pullam, provided inspiration along the way.

Introduction: Do You Want to Hear from God?

When I turned 50, I had an epiphany. I had always been big on setting goals and planning my next big thing. Then at age 50, it occurred to me that I might only have about 25 or 30 years left to do whatever needed to be done. Maybe less.

I suppose I'm not the only one to think such thoughts. Hence, we now have the famous bucket lists that many of my friends are creating. Would it surprise you to find out that most of those lists are filled with exotic places to visit? (I certainly want to go to Eastern Europe and Australia) The lists might include a new place to live, a certain car to own, or achieving some level of expertise in a sport or game. My conversations with others on the subject commonly come around to amassing some amount of net worth that will allow them to at least maintain their current standard of living.

It is very unlikely that many of those lists include the decision "doing whatever God calls me to do." Can you imagine how the rest of your life might look if you made that decision today? Whether you are 18, 30, or ancient of days like me, you could make a major impact in the days left to you.

Are you too busy? Are you worried about money? Do you think you do not possess the needed skills? Do you doubt you know what to do? Does it seem too big? Will you miss your TV too much? Are you afraid your family and friends will think you are weird? If you answered yes to any of those questions, then you are missing the Jesus that Paul, John, Matthew, Mark, James, Luke, Peter, and Jude talk about.

I'm not a special person. I'm a layman like most of you. I have prospered in life, but 5 years ago I lost almost everything and had to start over at age 60. I have some talents and skills, as do you. I wish I had more talents and skills, just as you do.

I do know this: if only one out of every 100 people that love Jesus in the US made a decision today to "do whatever God calls me to do" for the rest of their lives, this country and the world could experience revival unlike any other. Are you going to sit by and let someone else be that "one" who will enjoy all the fun, all the amazing best that God has to offer you while here on earth and then in heaven?

To take up God's call requires a lot of hard work, determination, and most of all, faith. Remarkably, if it really is God's call, and you respond with your whole heart, the yoke will seem light as a feather.

Seniors, you can choose to kick back and start counting the sunsets. You deserve it. You've worked hard, and now it is someone else's turn. Is that where you are?

On the other hand, maybe you're a young go-getter and you want treasures and fame here on earth. You might be promising God that you will use your money and fame to further the Kingdom later. I can identify with that very easily. Is this you?

Possibly, you have been badly wounded by life, and you're struggling to put one foot in front of the other. You think God can use you later. Are you hiding behind your wounds?

Do you think, "I'll do it when the kids are grown and through college. I'll surrender to God's call on my life when I have $500,000 in net assets." Do you think that God dare not call a parent with small children?

How do I know you think that way? Easy. I have thought those thoughts.

We need a revival in the US, and throughout the world. The ability to communicate the Gospel to every person on earth has never been easier. The world has never been more ready to hear the message. Unless you are missing the news, you probably think we are certainly in the last days. There isn't a lot of time left to make sure your loved ones and those in your community have Christ in their hearts.

If you are ready to commit to God fully and avoid any potential of being seen as lukewarm, this book is the outpouring of my heart intended to provide you with a pathway to victory.

Here is an outline of the path. Each step is based on a decision. Just like your initial decision to follow Jesus, you will be making decisions throughout your walk.

- Decision: That I will listen to God for His call on my life.

- Decision: That I will do what is necessary to hear and obey God's call on my life.

- Decision: That in order to be in a position to hear God's calling, I will love Him and others, and seek the intimacy that accompanies that love. I hunger and thirst for a right relationship with Him and others.

- Decision: That in order to love like that, I will be poor in spirit and more humble. Humility means that I trust God for my direction, not myself or other people. I believe what God says.

- Decision: I will become a disciple of Christ, which means watching and hearing what He teaches, then doing those things.

The Bible describes five kinds of followers of Jesus: the multitudes (Matt. 4:25), casual inquirers (John 4:9), disciples (Matt. 5:1), close disciples such as Peter, James, and John (Matt. 17:1), and an intimately close disciple (John 13:23). Which kind of follower are you?

The *multitudes* blend into the crowds on Sunday mornings. Rejecting service opportunities. Giving intermittently. Avoiding relationships. Avoiding commitment. They like being part of the crowd that gets close enough to Jesus to mollify the yearning desire in their hearts for relationship with Him, but not so close that His expectations touch them.

The *casual inquirers* ask endless questions about inconsequential matters. Seldom do they change their attitudes about the Lord but, rather, they relish the dispute and disagreements.

The *disciples* change the direction of their lives. They turn and follow Jesus after their encounter with Him. They learn from Him, they serve Him, they testify to what He's done in their lives, they share His love with others, and they stay close to Him. Even when they drift away and wander off, they eventually turn around and come back to a close relationship and fellowship with Jesus.

The best picture of the *intimate disciple* is John reclining against Jesus with his head on Jesus' breast. Do you think John heard Jesus' heart beat? I do. And I want to be *that* disciple--the one that is so close to Jesus that I hear His heartbeat. Do you? I believe you can be!

You can be the kind of disciple who is so close to Jesus that there is no room for anything to come between Him and you. The kind of disciple that worships Him as closely and intimately as humanly possible. The kind of disciple that hears God's voice distinctly calling to His service. The kind of disciple that, upon hearing God's call, answers: "Here am I. Send me."

Chapter 1—Be a Disciple

Millions of Christians across our globe say they love Jesus and believe the Bible. More millions convert each year. Many of those are also disciples of Christ. Sadly that number is not nearly what it could be.

There is not a verse in the Bible where Jesus or any of His disciples command those who believe to go out and make converts. The command is always to make disciples. In fact, Jesus pruned the crowds that followed Him of those who were not willing to do the hard things.

If the church were made up of even ten percent true disciples, based on the definition given by Jesus in Luke 14:25-33 (quoted below), it is easy to imagine how the world might be turned upside down.

Let's be real with one another. I know many Christian brothers and sisters who are truly good folks. They attend, give, possibly read their Bible, and pray. Some are even part of the work of the church.

Others are much more serious. They serve on two committees, always show up for work days, read their Bibles, pray every day, and give faithfully to their local church.

I know folks like that, and I've been that person. However, that description would not make someone a disciple, not according to the definition given us by Jesus. Here are the relevant Scriptures:

> *Then the eleven disciples went to Galilee, to the mountain where Jesus had told them to go. When they saw him, they worshiped him; but some doubted. Then Jesus came to them and said, "All authority in heaven and on earth has been given to me. Therefore go and make disciples of all nations, baptizing them in the name of the Father and of the Son and of the Holy Spirit, and teaching them to obey everything I have commanded you. And surely I am with you always, to the very end of the age.*

Matthew 28:16-20

> *Large crowds were traveling with Jesus, and turning to them he said:*
> *"If anyone comes to me and does not hate father and mother, wife and children, brothers and sisters—yes, even their own life—such a person cannot be my disciple. And whoever does not carry their cross and follow me cannot be my disciple. "Suppose one of you wants to build a tower. Won't you first sit down and estimate the cost to see if you have enough money to complete it? For if you lay the foundation and are not able to finish it, everyone who sees it will ridicule you, saying, 'This person began to build and wasn't able to finish.'*
>
> *"Or suppose a king is about to go to war against another king. Won't he first sit down and consider whether he is able with ten thousand men to oppose the one coming against him with twenty thousand? If he is not able, he will send a*

delegation while the other is still a long way off and will ask for terms of peace. In the same way, those of you who do not give up everything you have cannot be my disciples.

Luke 14:25–33

DISCIPLES GIVE UP EVERYTHING

These texts make it clear that to be a disciple one must:

- Obey everything that Jesus taught
- Hate his relatives (by comparison to his love for Christ)
- Carry Christ's Cross
- Give up everything

That certainly leaves me out. What about you? On the other hand, I'm not certain that Jesus intended for us to have achieved all of those things before we can be disciples. I do believe he intends for us to make a clear decision that we want to do these things, and that we will be available to do these things when called.

If we review the lives of both Old and New Testament saints, they did not give up everything every day or every week. Rather, they were available to give up whatever was necessary to respond to God's call. They were learning how to do those four things.

Jesus spent three years training the Twelve virtually full time how to be disciples. One could argue that even our seminaries spend more time on theology and counseling than they do on developing disciples. In order to "create disciples" so that there will be enough workers to gather the abundant harvest, the church may need to become much more proactive about specifically doing the necessary work to equip willing followers to be disciples.

Disciples Create Miracles

Very truly I tell you, whoever believes in me will do the works I have been doing, and they will do even greater things than these, because I am going to the Father.

John 14:12

Was this statement by Jesus intended to be taken literally? Some think not. However, let's examine a few miracles that have taken place over just the past few years. I submit to you that the forces behind these miracles are exactly as Jesus had intended: fully committed disciples who answered His call on their lives.

Campus Crusade for Christ

One couple, Bill and Vonette Bright made a decision early in their marriage to spend the rest of their lives doing whatever God called them to do.

While Bill Bright was a student at Fuller Theological Seminaries he felt the call of God to help fulfill Christ's Great Commission (Matthew 28:19). His first effort began with students at UCLA. This humble beginning became the largest evangelical effort ever, Campus Crusade for Christ.

From one couple's commitment arose Campus Crusade for Christ, which today has more than 27,000 full-time staff and over 225,000 trained volunteer staff in 191 countries.

Bill Bright produced the film *Jesus* in 1979. Pastor Rick Warren, author of *The Purpose Driven Life,* said this about the film: "The *Jesus* film is the most effective evangelistic tool ever invented."

According to Campus Crusade for Christ, more than 3.8 million per people make decisions to follow Christ every year after watching the *Jesus* movie. That's as if the population of the entire city of Los Angeles came to Christ each year.

One couple, fully devoted to Christ, answered a call, and they accomplished more than the original apostles, just as Jesus promised would happen.

Prison Fellowship

Chuck Colson made a decision to trust Jesus and to follow a calling.

Most Americans will remember Chuck Colson as one of President Nixon's hatchet man. He was named as one of the Watergate Seven because of his involvement in the famous Watergate burglary. Colson pled guilty to obstruction of justice and to defamation of Daniel Ellsberg, the reporter who broke the story of the Pentagon Papers. Colson eventually served seven months in the Federal Prison Camp in Montgomery, Alabama.

While mired in this crisis, Colson accepted Christ, a decision which abruptly and radically altered his life. The time spent in prison inspired and nurtured concern for those he met there. He founded Prison Fellowship. According to Wikipedia, Prison Fellowship is today, "the nation's largest outreach to prisoners, ex-prisoners, and their families." Colson worked to promote prisoner rehabilitation and reform of the prison system in the United States, citing his disdain for what he called the "lock 'em and leave 'em" warehousing approach to criminal justice. He helped to create prisons whose populations are restricted to inmates who choose to participate in faith-based programs.

Chuck Colson also authored 30 books after his conversion experience. Many of those books touched my heart greatly, including *The Body*, which became an instant Christian classic.

Chuck Colson was disgraced and imprisoned for his actions, and easily could have stayed out of the limelight for the rest of his days. God put a calling on his life, and the results can only be described as supernatural.

God Called

FOCUS ON THE FAMILY

After leaving a very successful career as a psychologist, Dr. James Dobson started a little radio program that was destined to affect millions.

Focus on the Family began in 1977 in a small office. By the time he stepped down in 2003, his radio show was reaching 220 million people daily in 164 countries. The program was also carried by 60 television stations in the US.

Dobson is a prolific author with several best-selling books aimed at helping families improve their marriages and parenting skills.

Under Dobson, the Focus on the Family campus in Colorado Springs employed over a thousand people who worked on outreach ministries that grew out of the radio program. These ministries were then, and are today, aimed at specific demographics including teenage boys and girls, children, college students, families, young adults, parents, while others are aimed at specific concerns, such as sexual problems, entertainment, and politics. Many have their own regular publications.

Were these individuals extraordinary? Certainly they had talents and intelligence, but so do millions of others who have not surrendered all. Is it necessary to have amazing gifts to be used by God in ways that are supernatural? Not at all. God has shown repeatedly in the Bible that he is perfectly capable of using people like you and me to do miraculous things.

YOU CAN BE A DISCIPLE

Are you satisfied to do for Jesus only what you can comfortably do with your own power? Too many Christians are. Are you willing to surrender everything and answer God by saying, "Send me," as Isaiah did? (Isaiah 6:8)

Much of what is offered here will seem too hard to those who have not chosen to make basic Christian disciplines a priority. Those who find this statement harsh must prepare for even greater challenges later in the book.

Many believers are not that interested in hearing from God, or in the surrender necessary to follow His calling. Only 5% of evangelical Christians even tithe. This does not mean that giving is a clear indicator of how serious you are about your Christian life, how much you trust God, or how strongly you believe the Bible. However, if God puts a serious call on your life, you are likely to be required to sacrifice a great deal more than merely meeting the Biblical standard for a minimum offering. The journey that awaits you is not for everyone. There are three very specific criteria that can help you determine whether you want to continue to read this book.

First, you must be a born-again believer in Jesus Christ. You must have recognized that you were a sinner. You must have offered up your repentance and asked Jesus to come into your life as Master. You must have understood that you are making a decision to leave the world behind and enter into eternal life.

Second, this journey is for mature Christians who have good familiarity with at least the New Testament, Psalms, Proverbs, Genesis, and the history around the founding fathers of the Jews. Paul (1 Corinthians 3:1-4) spoke of believers starting out with milk to drink and later graduating to meat. These metaphors illustrate various levels of spiritual maturity and ability to understand and respond to the Scriptures. Paul meant that believers would naturally mature as they put more effort into reading and studying the Bible.

Third, if you are not presently willing to respond to a call from God but do have a strong desire to move further along your spiritual pathway, you should read the book slowly. Stop along the way, making necessary changes in your life, repenting of your ongoing sinfulness, and opening yourself up to discover what it means to be truly committed to Jesus.

The book was written to share a layman's perspective on the journey to a place where you will mean it when you next sing "I Surrender All." If that describes what you are seeking, my prayer is that you will find this material helpful.

If you have *not* been saved by grace, through faith, and not by any work of your hand, but you feel that you want to hear from God, draw closer to Him, and enter into relationship with Him, please go immediately to: http://bit.ly/gospel-7 and learn about the incredible good news that is Christ Jesus.

GOD WANTS TO TALK WITH YOU

Both the Old Testament and the New Testament teach God's nature, truth, grace, and the themes of love, forgiveness, and sacrifice. The Old Testament approaches all of these things from the standpoint of the law, while the New Testament explains how Christ fulfills the law and thus frees us from the law. You will never fully understand God's plan, His goals for you, or His purposes until you have carefully and fully studied the Old Testament. St. Augustine said, "The New is in the Old Concealed, the Old is in the New Revealed." (*Novum Testamentum in Vetere latet, Vetus Testamentum in Novo patet*).[1] However, in both cases the purpose of God is the same: That we might live life abundantly. (See John 10:10)

In the Old Testament, we read that God declares the law in order that we may know how to live the best possible life. The Scriptures repeat that if we obey the law, things will go well with us. If we choose to disobey, the consequences will range from missing God's best gifts to very dire. The Old Testament makes it clear that God does not need our obedience. He commands it because He has created us and knows what will be best for us.

In the New Testament, the theme is even more pronounced, with hundreds of specific commands and directions for living the most blessed life on earth while preparing for the greatest rewards in heaven. Charles Spurgeon had a gift for explaining the blessed life in his series of 8 sermons on the Beatitudes. You can hear some of his sermons, including those on the Beatitudes at YouTube here: http://bit.ly/Beatitudes1

How can we achieve the greatest blessings if we are not willing to put aside earthly temptations and worldly desires in order to seek God and His call on our lives?

In his seminal work, *Hearing God*, Dallas Willard says,

Those who really do not want to hear what God has to say -- no matter what they may say to the contrary -- will position themselves before God in such a way 'that they may indeed look, but not perceive, and may indeed listen, but not understand; so that they may not turn again and be forgiven' (Mk 4:12). If we do not want to be converted from our chosen and habitual ways, if we really want to run our own lives without any interference from God, our very perceptual mechanisms will filter out his voice or twist it to our own purposes.

The doleful reality is that very few human beings really do concretely desire to hear what God has to say to them..."

..."our failure to hear his voice when we want to is due to the fact that we do not in general want to hear it, that we want it only when we think we need it.[2]

My personal experience is that few Christians have given any thought to hearing God's voice, and are not seeking to do so, except in crisis, as noted by Dallas Willard. Nevertheless, if you want the best that God has to offer now and in eternity, you need to seek His voice and become a sheep who recognizes the voice of your good Shepherd.

In the pages that follow, we will look at foundational principles of the Christian walk. They are critical if you intend to learn to understand God in loving intimacy that opens the communication pathways. We will talk about what it means to love and to be intimate with humans and with God. We will explore Christian disciplines and why being disciplined in the right way and attitude matters so much in the pursuit of Holiness.

Then we will address the most likely block to your spiritual growth—failure to forgive—and why this one aspect of our lives can be so devastating on so many levels. This material will be part of a section that also uncovers why some in the faith have difficulty with praise and/or asking. Repentance, as a continuing requirement of the Christian walk, wraps up this chapter in a way that intentionally prepares the reader for steps they may never have contemplated.

The next step is to investigate how we can hear from God. The intention of this chapter is to break down misconceptions about God's ability to speak to us the way he spoke to people in the Bible. We don't want to put God into any boxes that prevent communication with Him.

The final two chapters get to the meat of the issue: surrender and holiness. By this point in the book, many will be ready to hear from God, and these last chapters will be preparation for responding to God's call by saying, "Send me."

If only a small percentage of Christians tithe, and another small percentage study their Bible daily, it is easy to suspect that an even smaller percentage are disciplined in other ways. The numbers must necessarily diminish even further regarding those who repent on a regular basis. It follows that only a miniscule number are prepared to hear from God in a meaningful way. Isaiah 6:8 suggests that God was looking all over the place, plaintively calling out, "Who will go for us?" over and over, looking for even one person who would do what he asked. You can be that one who is prepared to answer God's call with "Here am I. Send me."

Feature Story--Follow God's Clear Call

I surrender all, I surrender all,
All to Thee, my bless'd Savior,
I surrender all.

In 1992, I enjoyed a period of time when my Christian discipline was at a peak. I was serving God as best I knew how and desiring to do more. I had even recognized and dealt with (at some level) the big stumbling block of being proud of my devotion and service compared to others. Of course, none of that made me "perfect" in my day-to-day walk. Good discipline should dramatically affect our Holiness when we are that fully committed, but we are still just sinful humans.

In the course of my reading at that time, I was trying to move towards surrender. The great hymn, "I Surrender All" haunted me every time I sang it. I knew I didn't surrender all. In 1992, I experienced an important revelation.

In my prayer time I told God I was ready to go anywhere, do anything, even uproot my family . . . anything that He wanted me to do to serve Him. I was trying to say "Send me." However, when I prayed these words thinking I meant them, I added at the end: "Except Haiti!" I meant that, too. I had been in Haiti, known others who had been missionaries to Haiti, and I never wanted to spend even one more hour there.

Then one morning I changed the prayer. I was probably affected by the Abraham/Isaac story. God would not ask me to go to Haiti unless it was going to be a huge blessing. I finally prayed a prayer of complete surrender and added: "Even Haiti."

Not long after that prayer was first offered, then repeated,

God Called

I got into a minor spat with my wife, Pam, just before bed. We turned out the light, and the chill in the room was nothing that could be changed by turning up the heater. After a bit, I prayed over that fight in a way I was not accustomed to doing. I prayed for God's clear voice as to what I was to do regarding the fight.

God clearly told me I was to ask her to forgive me. Then He immediately changed the subject. In the next hour or so, he laid out a project in such detail that it was breathtaking. The project was not anything that was remotely on my radar, though the subject was on my heart then, and now. It was a subject that I had studied about 20 years before while in college.

THE CALL

God said that I was to write a book entitled *Sex Kills*. He laid out the format for the book, chapter titles, and details of what the book was to include. He further indicated that the book was to be completed in time for the Promise Keepers Convention the following summer, less than nine months away. I had just sold a book to a major national publisher, and knew that researching, writing, finding a publisher, and getting a book printed in that time frame would be virtually impossible, even if I were free to do it full time. However, I was running a company and had a family of five. My days were full.

The details prescribed were enough to make me believe it was clearly from God. I heard no "audible" voice, but I heard God. The conversation was like having a conversation with a friend. I argued with God about the timing, and He made it clear that this was the timing He required.

What unfolded in the following nine months is just as amazing as the source of the call. Over and over the clear intention and intervention of God was obvious to all who were involved.

I used every spare minute to research and to begin to outline and write the book. This was just before the dawn of the internet age, so every bit of the research had to be done at libraries. I spent most of my lunch hours at the local library, searching for the details that I needed for the book.

Of course, there is more to writing a book than merely research and writing. There is editing, rewriting, and finding a publisher. Finding a publisher was the first major test of faith and that search gave me evidence of God at work.

I honestly had no idea how any publisher would be able to take the book through multiple edits, format the final effort, create a cover, then plan and execute the printing in less than six months.

As the writing of the first draft took me into March, I was at a crossroads. There were only 120 days until the Promise Keepers convention, and I had not found a publisher.

Months before I had asked my agent to present the new book idea to Warner Books. Warner had just bought a book from me, so this was the obvious first choice. They also had a Christian division. I put together a marketing proposal and sent it to the editor. He rejected the project. In fact, he was upset that I would be losing focus trying to promote two books at once.

I went back to my agent and asked for her direction and opinion. She was unhappy that I was splitting my time and energy in such diverse directions. She suggested that it would be much better for my career if I concentrated on one type of writing, especially since writing was only a part-time effort. In other words, she did not help me at all.

Next I started researching publishers and agents in the Christian book business. Most of the non-fiction agents were handling major writers, and I made no progress. I was truly puzzled. I had just sold a book to Warner. I should have been a hot property. Besides, God was in my corner.

DECISION TO SELF-PUBLISH

Time was passing quickly. I decided that I needed to be prepared to self-publish. I had not done that before and had no idea where to turn. More research. I set a date of March 31. If I did not find a publisher by then, I would do it myself.

As I was fully engaged in finding a publisher for *Sex Kills*, the Warner book arrived on the shelves, and Warner expected me to help publicize it. It received a few reviews. I was booked for a radio show or two and one minor cable TV program. I really wanted a chance to be heard on KKLA, a Christian talk radio station in LA. My goal was to appear during the evening drive time.

I wrote and called the evening drive time host and finally had a conversation with him. Unfortunately, he did not see how a book about starting and running a small business would really fit his audience.

Then I tell him about *Sex Kills*. I promised to give him the inaugural interview on that book if he let me talk about the business book. He asked me to overnight a copy to his office. I sent it, and he agreed to the deal.

The Radio Interview

I did the interview live at the station, since I live only a few miles away. I had planned to tease the "Sex Kills" book during the interview, but I didn't yet know who would publish it. The interview went well, and I went back to my car. I turned on the radio to the same show so I could hear the next guest.

This guest had also just published a book. I'll never forget the title. *Gays and Guns.* That's almost all I remember about the book. The other thing I remember is the first ten minutes of the interview. It must have been very nearly the worst ten minutes in radio history. There could not have been three people listening to those ten minutes who were remotely interested in what was being discussed.

It seems this fellow had written a college thesis on "Gays and Guns." He had decided to sell it as a book, but he, too, was faced with some kind of deadline. He spent ten minutes telling the host how his publisher had been able to turn his book around and publish it in three months. It was hugely exciting for the author, but most of the audience probably had no idea that it normally took longer than that, or cared.

There was one listener in the audience who cared. I memorized the name of the publisher, Huntington House, as I drove home (no smartphone to jot a verbal note). Even though it was late when I arrived home that night, I asked myself, why not call anyway? I called, and a man answered. I explained that I was an author with a finished manuscript, and I said I wanted to talk to someone about publishing the book. He said that everyone else had gone home, and that he was the senior editor. Then he asked what the book was about.

As soon as I said *Sex Kills*, he immediately asked me to overnight a copy to him so that he could review it over the weekend. The next day he called to say that he was sending me a contract that would reach me on Monday. He had not waited until the weekend.

Twenty-four hours before this call, I did not even know where to try next for a publisher. Suddenly, I had a contract on the way. Moreover, this company was willing to do the book in less than 90 days. All of this transpired because I had listened to the worst ten minutes in radio history.

This series of events was implausible. A miracle? Maybe not. What makes a surprise into a miracle? Still, it did seem to be a God thing. And there is more!

THE CHOICE

True to their word, Huntington House acted immediately. Soon editors were sending me blood red manuscripts in place of the black and white I had sent them. It did not seem possible, but the project was moving rapidly forward.

Believing firmly that God wanted my book to be available at the Promise Keepers event, I tried to register for a booth. My application was rejected. There was no room for me or my ads or promotional materials. However, I kept the faith that God had a reason for the timing. Then I got the first call that tested everything, and I flunked the test.

The call came from the Huntington House senior editor. He and his sales manager had been pitching the book to some of their best Christian bookstore customers, and there was universal interest in the book... BUT and it was a big but, they hated the title. One and all said the book would not do well in a Christian bookstore in 1993 with the word *sex* in the title.

His team had worked on a new title. He asked how I liked *A Generation Betrayed: It's Time to End the Sexual Revolution*. I don't do titles. I write books. Others do my titles. In this case God gave me the title. We argued. He said that the deal was off if I stuck with the title. *I didn't consult God!* I made the decision to go forward with the new title in order to make the deadline.

Shortly after that conversation, I received another bad news phone call. The Christian Bookseller's Convention was also coming up in August, and there was not a printing press in the USA that could take my book in time for the Promise Keepers convention, also scheduled for August. Major publishers had reserved every press in order to have their books in stock for the bookseller's convention.

Did God intend these two setbacks as a test of my faith? I'll never know. I do know that I was charging full steam ahead.

The failure

I have published eight books. Six have been very successful. One was okay, but not great. This book was a complete disaster. It sold less than 1000 copies. Most of those were sold from my book table at speaking engagements. To this day, I believe that if the title had been *Sex Kills*, the book would have sold very well. Oh, did I mention that the cover art was worse than the title? See the illustration above.

The outcome

Huntington House, the publisher, may or may not have been good at titles or covers, but they were gifted at publicity. From the very first conversation about my contract, they informed me that I needed to be prepared to give lots of interviews, mostly radio talk shows. This was their method for selling books.

They were good indeed. In the next year, I was interviewed on more than 200 radio shows. God's message was broadcast widely. These radio shows were often secular shows, and the callers frequently rejected the biblical concepts in the book vehemently.

The reason we got so many requests for interviews was an ad that the publisher placed in a talk show magazine. The headline . . . go ahead and see if you can guess . . . "Sex Kills." Some of these shows had a few thousand listeners. Some might have had 100,000 or more. Then one day we received a call from Geraldo's daytime TV show.

They were doing a show on bisexuality, and needed an expert guest to speak against it. We agreed to do the show. Within hours we had a call from Montel Williams who wanted to do an interview about the book. We said "sure." Unfortunately, when Montel heard that we were already booked on Geraldo, that deal was off.

So, off to New York and the limo and the green room I went. The show featured three bisexual young adults from the Seattle area, Geraldo, and me. I was the only one to speak against bisexuality. The show was seen by several million, then aired in repeat at least five times that we know of. Millions and millions heard the book's message, even though Geraldo only booked me because the ad said "Sex Kills." The book cover was shown on the screen to those same millions, but the book still did not sell.

Some might look at that entire story and say, "interesting set of coincidences." It would be easier to agree with that observation if the origin of the idea had not been God's direction during prayer. I believe that it was all orchestrated to make a statement to the budding bisexuality movement, and to speak to millions of others on radio about Biblical foundations of sexual purity. Many other voices were speaking out at that time, including Promise Keepers and the entire purity ring movement.

The tide actually turned in 1994, the year after these events. There were fewer high school pregnancies and their seemed to be an awakening about STDs and the other negative consequences of sex outside of marriage. In 2013, the waters are rising once again. If God wants me to do a rewrite, the title is definitely going to be whatever He says it should be.

Chapter 2—Go For Him

A scroll of the Book of Isaiah.

I would like to invite you on a journey. Not unlike the journey of Bilbo Baggins of *The Hobbit* and *Lord of the Rings* fame, the journey is also an adventure. I will encourage but never coerce you to take this journey, but I believe that I can promise you only good will come from it. On the other hand, on the way to gaining that good, there could easily be trials, danger, impossible choices, and obstacles that seem insurmountable. Just as it was for Bilbo Baggins.

Since you will be seeking to hear from God and ultimately to find out His will for you or His calling for your life, the Devil is very likely to make an effort to stop you. The last thing that the Devil wants is for Christ' followers actually to do the will of the Father, or imitate the life of the Son, or be filled by the Holy Spirit.

I have chosen to follow this path to the point of complete surrender to God's call on only two occasions. Once I did this successfully, at least in my proud mind. The other time the results were very unsuccessful, indeed, at least in my proud mind. The first story is featured between chapters 1 and 2. The second story will be told later in the book, between chapters 7 and 8.

GOD CAN USE YOU IN MIRACULOUS WAYS

Could God use you in a surprising way? If you believe the Bible is the word of God, then you necessarily believe that every person who believes in Him is blessed with abundant gifts that could and should be used by Him for kingdom purposes.

Do you need a specific calling on your life in order to be useful in some form of ministry? No. Parenting is ministry. Serving other Christians through greeting worshipers is a ministry. Teaching, tithing, or supporting your pastor, church, brothers and sisters in prayer are all ministries many Christians perform as naturally as they breathe.

Some also feel led to help feed the homeless or work in a home for unwed mothers or do street evangelism. They work as faithful servants of God without ever having felt a special calling. Yet, the tug on their hearts to work in such ministries is evidence of God's leadership in their lives.

However, Christians might also choose to serve in any of the above ways to fill their own needs, to feel important, to try to earn their salvation, to be seen as helpful, to impress some organizer, or simply to get closer to someone they care about.

All of these motives can be a minor incentive or the main reason. Each person must examine his motives for acting, which may not be the same thing as a calling.

How do you know what God wants you to do? If the work you think you are doing for God feels like drudgery, then it probably is not from God. If you love the attention, the accolades, or the appreciation more than the blessing you give to others, you might want to question your motivation. How can you know with confidence that you are answering God's call?

The Scriptures show you how to hear and how to respond to a call from the Lord in ways that delight both Him and you.

THE ISAIAH 6:8 CALLING

The path ahead, or journey, or adventure that I will show you in this book is based on Isaiah 6:8 and other Scriptures. This is not the only way to hear from God. God is not limited in his ability to call you if you do not follow this guide. Rather, it is my experience of one way to hear God and then to act. As I laid out this path, I asked others who are spiritually mature to challenge it in every way. Their insight added perspective to my own experience which is the foundation for this book. If my experience is helpful to you, then we both are blessed.

Some people prefer a guidebook, a map, or a GPS turn-by-turn navigation system to help them reach their destination. Others like to bump along making wrong turns and running into dead ends while they work on the path like a maze. This guidebook is designed more for the first, who might keep it handy to check out the next landmark. For the latter, it might be a quick read that gets them started, but leaves them free to discover their own variations on this theme.

Chapter 3—Hear His Voice

The Foundation is love of God and others

I personally struggle with two words more than any others in the English language: *intimacy* and *love*. I have believed myself to be in love several times, especially as a teenager. It is ironic that in high school I even wrote a paper on the subject. I was quite impressed with it, actually, but when I was required to read it aloud, my classmates laughed until they cried, while I turned red as a beet.

In recent months I have begun to understand just a bit of each of these words. I am thankful that it has happened as I am becoming reacquainted with God. This recommitment comes after a period of frustration with His *allowing* a very rough patch in my world.

Tim Keller, in his beautiful and charming work, *King's Cross*, showed me how my pride and lack of faith were serious issues. As I started dealing with these problems, I restarted an adventure from which I detoured five years earlier. With that background, I offer my feeble and terribly new understanding of intimacy.

In order for any of us to be able to listen fully to another, we must know that person profoundly. When we know someone deeply, we can hear what their heart is saying, even beyond what their words are expressing. Knowledge of the other person becomes deeper and deeper when each is able to share their innermost feelings with trust. The more trust, the more depth of sharing, and the more intimate the relationship.

My youngest grandchild is two. We all know what that means. Frustration builds upon frustration due to her inability to express fully what is going on inside. The frustration often explodes in ways that destroy the peace of anyone within earshot. It can bring grown men and tenderhearted women to panic and quite inappropriate decisions. Yet somehow most parents, grandparents, even older siblings, learn to know the causes of the meltdowns. Somehow the terrible twos melt into a time when the child is better able to express her feelings and hurts and needs. Somehow everyone in her world starts to understand her better, and the result is a growing closeness coupled with a reduction in the stress for everyone.

You may have also experienced something like this in a retreat or overnight stays with friends when you were young - talking all night, divulging secrets, and learning about one another.

We could stay transparent about our feelings as we grow up, and we could learn from the success that accompanied being open and talking it through. Sadly, we actually start to withhold almost as quickly as we trusted. We fear being wrong or losing the love of our siblings. We fear being manipulated. The risks of transparency feel weightier than the potential rewards.

Later we will take risks again. Now and then, we risk vulnerability with our parents or other relatives. Sometimes we dare risk it with friends, with those who teach us, or with those we teach. Then we learn it all over again in our dating, courting, and married lives.

FEAR CRUSHES LOVE

We Desire to Know and Be Known.
We Fear Knowing and Being Known

The common thread is the desire to know and be known. The common difficulty is the fear of knowing or being known. Our desires and fears can be summed up in the word *vulnerable*. We desire the closeness that being vulnerable produces, but we are held back by the pain that we feel when people we trust belittle our weaknesses, our old wounds, or our deepest thoughts.

Therefore, just as with any other relationship, the journey to deepest intimacy with God begins as we make His acquaintance. The better we know and understand God, the more we will be able to understand what He is saying to us through His word, through the teaching of others, or through His still, small voice.

It sounds almost irreverent, but as with any intimate relationship, we must be prepared to accept God no matter what. He will appear to have "flaws" that we can't understand. How could He let babies die? Why did He bring the flood? Why didn't He make Bobby Smith love me? Why did He let my favorite aunt get cancer?

Likewise, we must be prepared to open up our darkest rooms, trust Him with our weird thoughts, and forgive Him when his timing is not the same as ours, or when He says "no," or if we have losses in life. There's that word *vulnerable* again. We struggle to remain vulnerable as we attempt to believe that it is safe to expose ourselves to God and to trust Him completely.

In order to know God this intimately, we will need to study Him, spend time with Him, engage with Him, and build up our trust in Him. That is where we begin.

Chapter 4--Be Intimate

The Bible used by Abraham Lincoln for his oath of office during his first inauguration in 1861.

READ YOUR BIBLE

"I'm not *that* religious."
I spoke with an associate one day who told me, "I believe, but I'm not religious." That was not the first time I had heard someone say that. In fact, I personally might have felt exactly the same for all of my twenties and into my thirties. Maybe you have heard the same thing from friends or felt the same way at times.

My associate happens to be someone who has very strong beliefs in many areas of her life, including a conviction that GMOs (genetically modified organisms) are dangerous and should never be eaten, nor should we eat the meat from animals that have ingested GMO corn or other food products.

She is not a scientist, but has widely read the online literature on the subject. Through this reading, she has come to trust those who insist that the chemical companies are knowingly providing various seed stocks to farmers that they know will cause harm to animals and people. She trusts this information, and is prepared to argue for hours that it is true.

I ask her to consider two ideas. One: science finds out that it is wrong about some earlier notion, headline theory, or prediction pretty much every day. Sometimes it is just the small stuff, like the Alar scare, or fear that cranberry juice will cause cancer. Other times it is on much larger issues, such as the origin and nature of the universe or the origin of life, the scientific explanations for which have been completely revised multiple times in the last 60 years.

I am amazed at her profound trust of science, especially when I note that the science is not even remotely settled. She is quite willing to change her diet, carefully study labels, question restaurants, and pay extra for food that is supposedly GMO free. She may turn out to be right. I have no idea, but right or wrong, she is not alone in her belief, or in the intensity of her belief. Millions of citizens with even less scientific understanding or even less exposure to the subject have the same view. That is certainly great faith. These people are quite religious on this subject.

I then propose that she think about another idea: Two: many prophecies in the Bible can be demonstrated to have been fulfilled. Over long periods of time they were shown to be true. In the Old Testament God told Abraham:

> *I will make you into a great nation, and I will bless you; I will make your name great, and you will be a blessing.*
> Genesis 12:2

Then Ishmael. The angel told his mother Hagar:

"I will increase your descendants so much that they will be too numerous to count."

Gen 16:10

If either of these two things had not happened, the Bible would be just another book. The world would simply point to the big miss on a critical issue, and the argument about the Bible being true, perfect, is over. The fact that almost half of the world's population is descended from these two men either biologically or spiritually is amazing indeed.

The Old Testament is quite clear that the Jews, a very small religious sect, would be scattered all over the earth, and would later be restored to Israel. In 1948 the Jews, the very subjects of the prophecy, gathered in Israel and became a state. This took place after the Jews had been scattered and persecuted for 2500 years. These miraculous prophecies are just a few of hundreds that have come true in great detail. Unlike science, which affirmed for centuries that the sun revolved around the earth only to discover that the opposite was true, biblical prophecy has been confirmed thousands of years after being written.

I asked why her faith was so strong in the science of these websites, but so weak when it comes to a source (The Bible) that has proven itself over many thousands of years. Why would she change her lifestyle on the basis of these authors and scientists she does not even know, but not change her lifestyle based on the Bible?

Do not doubt God

Then it occurred to me that all who believe could make the statement she made. We believe, but we aren't *that* religious. I mean that our faith is not complete. We may have enough faith to go to church or to pray during trouble or momentous events.

We may have enough faith to put some money in the offering, to help out a poor person, or to forgive someone who is not deserving of forgiveness.

However, we might not be faithful enough to be joyful in our giving, helping, or forgiving. We may be joyful in giving what we can afford, but not joyful about giving what would represent sacrifice. We may have the faith to keep us on a narrow path regarding stealing, but we might still think that gossip is not so bad. We don't really believe that seeking God's Kingdom first is more beneficial than a degree from a University or a business venture or an investment. We certainly do not have the faith to move mountains.

Do not feel like a failure

We need to be prepared to acknowledge that we are working under our own rules, ideas, assumptions, and attempting to "work" on our faults, rather than allowing the Holy Spirit to guide us. Why? Because we so often try to be our own source of our faith rather than ask the Father to give us the faith we need. We trust ourselves more than we trust God. Therefore, a major step on our journey, which we will need to repeat often, is the step of repentance.

How can we work on intimacy with God if we are not following His will even in the basics? It would be like trying to become intimate with a friend when our relationship was entirely superficial. Furthermore, how can we feed our heart, soul, and body with the right spiritual food if we aren't reading the Bible? We need to repent of our pride of self-sufficiency, and begin to meet with God on a regular basis by reading the Bible in order to get started on the right path.

Follow God in the basics

We do not need to speculate whether God wants us to read the Bible. If we believe the Bible is true, we can find dozens of specific statements in the Old and New Testaments about the importance of immersing ourselves in the Word of God. Examples include:

> *You study the Scriptures diligently because you think that in them you have eternal life. These are the very Scriptures that testify about me.*

John 5:39

> *I have not departed from your laws, for you yourself have taught me. How sweet are your words to my taste, sweeter than honey to my mouth! I gain understanding from your precepts; therefore I hate every wrong path. Your word is a lamp for my feet, a light on my path.*

Psalms 119: 102-105

While we can hear from God in many other ways, there is no clearer resource than the Bible. There is no more complete, detailed, deep, wide, well-written, easily digestible, way of hearing from God. We are promised that the Holy Spirit will help us to understand the Bible when we are confused. Teachers, preachers, and writers provide us with unlimited amounts of background and interpretation of the Bible. If we want to know God and hear from Him, the door could not be more wide open.

Which brings us back to the questions: "Do you want to hear from God? Do you want to hear his voice?" If you want to hear from God, you can. Any time of the day or night, for as many hours per day as you choose; in hundreds of languages, with notes to help you, and the Holy Spirit to guide you.

It seems hard to understand why we are "not that religious," but John reported it:

> *On hearing it, many of his disciples said, "This is a hard teaching. Who can accept it?"*
> *Aware that his disciples were grumbling about this,*

Jesus said to them, "Does this offend you? Then what if you see the Son of Man ascend to where he was before! The Spirit gives life; the flesh counts for nothing. The words I have spoken to you—they are full of the Spirit and life. Yet there are some of you who do not believe." For Jesus had known from the beginning which of them did not believe and who would betray him. He went on to say, "This is why I told you that no one can come to me unless the Father has enabled them."

From this time many of his disciples turned back and no longer followed him.

John 6:60-65

Too hard to accept, or just don't want to? The result is the same. We don't want to do what the Father has called us to do. We live on a merry-go-round. We don't read the Bible; therefore we don't trust God. We don't trust God; therefore, we don't read the Bible. We can't build trust without intimacy and so it goes, round and round.

If you want to hear what God has to say about you, your life, your eternal salvation, how to relate to others, and how to live life joyously now, and if you are excited about your future with

Him in heaven, then the journey starts with Bible reading. The more you read, the more you will understand God, be intimate with God, love God, trust God, and be willing to surrender to Him and His perfect will for your life.

Make a decision today. A commitment. A chapter a day. 20 pages a day. 15 minutes a day. Find a translation that works for you. The easiest of all is the *International Children's Bible*.[3] My kids learned to read using this Bible. It is a full translation at the 3rd grade reading level. It might be perfect for you. Another very easy read is *The Answer*, also known as the New Century Version.[4]

I'm reminded of bowling. If you try to learn to bowl while using a heavy ball, it takes all the fun out of the game and makes it hard to succeed. Learn with a lighter ball, and then use a heavier one after you learn your way around the game and learn some skills. Likewise, as you get acquainted with the Bible, find one that is fun to read and easy to understand as you develop the habit of Bible reading.

Chapter 5—Mature in Discipline

One of my favorite churches. Kihei, Maui.

JOIN A COMMUNITY OF BELIEVERS - THE CHURCH

How smart are you? How wise? How learned? How mature? Are you spiritually alive? Be honest. God says he wants us to be wise. He wants us to eat meat and not still live on milk. He calls us to be zealous, not lukewarm. He provides us with all the tools to achieve success in all of the above. Yet many who say they are Christ followers claim they do not need the tools he lays out for us. "We're doing just fine," they say.

Others simply do not want to be told what to do. I hate instructions. In particular I loathe Ikea furniture instructions, and surround sound instructions, and the instructions for other things that need to be hooked up to TV's. I would prefer never to open another instruction book. My male pride protests that I should be able to figure it out myself. I am even more defeated when I can't figure it out even with instructions.

Many, maybe including you, have that same approach when it comes to living this life and preparing for the next. You may acknowledge that God lays out in great detail the tools and methods he expects us to use in order to excel in life. You may agree that they sound right and all, but you excuse yourself saying, "Maybe next week I'll get around to it. Maybe when I'm really needy."

Why is the discipline of church participation so difficult for so many? Just about 85% of Americans claim to be followers of Jesus, claim to believe he is Lord, and call themselves Christian. Some are mouthing what they have always been told, but they don't have a clue about trusting Jesus as their savior. We all know folks who sound quite knowledgeable about Jesus and God, yet they say they don't want to be part of a church. They say they don't need to, or don't have time to, or can't work their schedule to, or they simply cannot find the right *church* to attend.

Now it is easy to find fault with "organized religion." It is even easier to be critical of specific pastors, denominations, or church bodies. It is extremely easy to find fault with the Christians who go to church. They are judgmental, hypocritical, easily led, and not living very much different day-to-day than the folks who don't go to church.

Those who reject churches because of the imperfect people who are members also have other requirements for the "perfect" church. It should fill their needs. It should not be asking for money all the time. It should leave the members in peace and not expect them to socialize with one another. It should have good music (meaning the kind they like), the seating should be comfortable, and the pastor should not preach a long time or run the service longer than an hour. They have lists, and they refuse to affiliate with a church that does not meet their requirements.

I have searched Scripture and I can't find a single verse that deals with churches filling the needs of the churched. I do see quite a few references to church being a place where we go to help those in need, meet together for prayer and remembrance, to teach and learn, and to lift our voices in praise together. I suppose you could work backward and figure that if the church exists in part to help those in need, that there must also be members in need. This is true. In fact, almost every member is or will be in need for the prayers, hands, feet, and words of their brothers and sisters in Jesus, but getting help isn't the reason we go. It is a benefit of our belonging.

The church is also the wellspring of outreach to the community for both service and evangelism. I rarely meet the person who is serving or evangelizing on their own, but not attending church. It happens, but very rarely.

Finally, though I am sure you could add to the list, where does the person not attending church pay their tithe? We are called to bring our tithe to the church. We are promised great blessings from doing so. The discipline of tithing is more likely to be lost when we are not a part of a body.

FIND GIFTED TEACHERS AND WISE COUNSELORS

For lack of guidance a nation falls, but victory is won through many advisers.

Proverbs 11:14

God commands us to sit under wise teachers and for some to be teachers. Part of the church experience includes sitting

under wise teachers, or having the gift of teaching. It seems that God did not think his Bible was all we would need to work out our Christian lives. Priests, judges, prophets, teachers, preachers, elders, apostles are just some of the job titles of teachers that God appoints to help us to greater understanding of His Word.

If you're anything like me, you hated school, even though you loved learning. Maybe you aren't like me and you loved school, but learning wasn't high on your list of fun things to do. Either way, God has made it abundantly clear that we need teachers, and never suggests that the learning process will be easy or fun.

Some of the critics of my writing in the business world say that I merely present common sense. I take that as a compliment, of course. However, they mean that I have not given them something new and exciting that will change everything they knew before. Yet the best selling book of all times by many multiples was completed 2000 years ago. Nothing is being added to it today. It is certainly all common sense, though some think we need something new because it is old fashioned.

2000 years old or not, it was created as a foundational guide to the best possible life on earth, and the direct path to heaven for those who choose to trust it. Foundational. Teachers add the walls, roof, and furnishings. If we are truly to know God, Jesus, and the Holy Spirit in the way God intends, we need to sit under solid Bible teachers. The Bible says, *"The way of fools seems right to them, but the wise listen to advice."* (Proverbs 12:15)

A note: The issue of following God's directions for our lives is a matter of faith and trust. We either have faith and trust that He is showing us the best possible way to live our lives, or we do not have that faith. If we have too little faith, it will keep us from receiving and giving all that God has in mind for us.

It goes to the very heart of our journey. Let's say you had someone under your direction, an employee, or an assistant. You gave them very specific directions which they then decided to disregard. When asked, they told you that they thought their way was better. In other words, they lacked faith in your method.

You might fire the person on the spot, or you might give them another chance. If they did the same thing a second time, you would be fairly foolish to continue to give them new assignments. You certainly would not give them a larger, more critical task.

It is the same with God. You say that you want to hear from Him, but if you do not read His Word, attend church, sit under good teaching, and accept His authority, you are already ignoring three of the ways He might talk to you. How can He talk to you about anything? The Bible makes it clear that when God gives people jobs, the going gets tough. If you are not doing the easy things, why should you expect Him to talk with you about the hard things?

You should think about this. If you are not busy with the easy jobs in the kingdom of God, how will you figure out what to do if God gives you a hard job? Why would He believe that you have the spiritual maturity to seek His direction or open your Bible to gain insight as to how to proceed? We need to show ourselves trustworthy in the small things in order to be offered the chance to handle bigger things. Don't expect to hear from God about a promotion if you are not doing the job you already have.

BUILD RELATIONSHIPS WITH STRONG DISCIPLES

The way of a fool is right in his own eyes, but a wise man listens to advice.

Proverbs 12:15

Where there is no guidance, a people falls, but in an abundance of counselors there is safety.

Proverbs 11:14

Listen to advice and accept instruction, that you may gain wisdom in the future. Many are the plans in the mind of a man, but it is the purpose of the Lord that will stand.

Proverbs 19:20-21

Plans fail for lack of counsel, but with many advisers they succeed.

Proverbs 15:22

God clearly intends us to be under the counsel of others. The Bible says that Solomon was the wisest person ever, and yet in his writings, he repeatedly states that seeking out wise counsel is necessary for safety, wisdom, and success. If the wisest man in history needed counsel, how could we think it is right for us to go through life without such counsel?

Where can we find such counselors? They are all around us. The Holy Spirit can use anyone as a resource for giving you great advice. However, you should do your part in choosing your advisors.

Personally, I seek out the advice of people who are mature in the Lord. If I plan to trust someone with my deepest and most critical issues, I want those people to be trustworthy, and not inclined towards gossip. I prefer individuals who have empathy for my circumstances. I want them to have lived through experiences similar to my situation. I look for someone who cares about me, and I want to know that my chosen advisor prays about me and for me and for my situation.

Experience has shown me that God will consistently provide these guides if I ask him to help me. I must do my part and seek them out. Then I need to listen carefully to their guidance. Finally, I should be prepared to actually do what they propose. If anyone advises me to disobey God, I know that this is not the advisor God prepared for me, but when God has provided good advisors, he expects me to learn from them.

I have had the experience of receiving conflicting advice on an important subject. One time in particular dealt with tithing. I was going through a difficult patch financially and didn't have enough income to pay the tithe. It was literally buy food or pay the tithe. Both advisors met all the criteria I outlined above, but their answers were directly opposite to each other. However, I had two respected views to consider. Their views were helpful in choosing a path. I determined that my first obligation was to buy food for my family. I picked up the tithe as quickly as I could, and feel the blessings of having been faithful.

When you are deeply involved in your church and have made friends who know you at a deep level, you generally have a brother or sister in the faith just a text message away. That person might be the voice of God that you need at that moment. If you are isolated, therefore not involved with other believers, God can still provide you with someone to fill this role, but be aware that your own part in the process becomes much more difficult. When you are a strong member of the body, you also become available to be a counselor when others need your direction.

Is it hard for you to ask others for advice? Do you seek advice and then listen half-heartedly? Or do you receive the advice of a wise counselor, only to disregard it in the end? These are all evidences of pride and a lack of faith in God's clear directions. You would be wise to repent of pride and lack of faith. Ask God to give you wisdom and to provide you with a circle of wise advisors.

I have invited you to travel with me on a journey, and the decision to go with me assumes that you want to hear the voice of God with clear directions for your life and your potential service for Him. If you don't have that desire, these disciplines and directions will still help you to live the best possible life and make the best preparation for heaven. If you do have that desire, these would be critical steps in moving you to the place where you hear God's voice.

Chapter 6—Trust Him Completely

If you plant a healthy seedling in good soil, provide it with proper light, water, and food the plant will almost always grow to maturity. The first five steps of a disciple's journey are very much like the life of that plant. If you read your Bible daily, pray daily, attend church regularly, sit under great teaching, and surround yourself with wise counsel, you will almost surely grow to maturity.

As a plant matures it begins to produce in the way God intended it to produce. This happens automatically unless there is disease, a predator, bad weather, or an accident.

The plant produces stems, leaves, flowers, fruit, and seeds. I'm not a botanist so please don't take my description too literally.

Each of these parts of the plant is necessary for health and maximum potential for providing what God intends. God might intend the plant to provide shelter to other living things, structure to the soil to prevent erosion, food for other creatures, beauty to be enjoyed by humans, seeds to produce future plants, and fertilizer for future purposes through death and decay.

So it is with humans and God's plan for them. As the Bible

clearly states, each person has different gifts and abilities so that they may make unique contributions to the Kingdom. As Christians mature and prepare for that purpose, how can they defend themselves from enemies, disease, mental or emotional distress, spiritual coldness or backsliding, unfortunate circumstances, accidents, and the Devil, himself?

It goes without saying that there are some things that cannot be avoided. The rain falls on the saved and the unsaved, the spiritually awesome and those who are barely hanging on. Nevertheless, most of the distractions and attacks Christians face can be met head on if they are fully prepared.

The disciplines already listed are part of the arsenal available to Christians during dark days. However, my understanding and experience is that there are at least four additional disciplines that will provide substantial additional armor against problems that will come:

- giving,
- sacrificing in love,
- fasting, and
- forgiving.

Each of these could be a book unto themselves, but for the purposes of this book, I will simply touch on each.

Give because everything belongs to God

There is every reason to believe that everything that could ever be said about giving and tithing has already been said. The very sad truth is that Christians give much less than a tithe of their earnings to God and other charities. Evangelicals give over 5% on average, but other Christian groups give less than that. All Christians give more than atheists, even to non-religious organizations and causes, but it is certainly not a tithe, and doesn't approach being sacrificial.

These statistics are a bit old, but later information shows little change. According to pollster, George Barna:

Although generosity, stewardship and tithing are higher profile issues among born again Christians than to other people, relatively few born again adults—only 9% - tithed to churches in 2004. That behavior was most common among evangelicals (23%), and much smaller among non-evangelical born again Christians (7%), notional Christians (less than 1%), people of other faiths (1%) and atheists and agnostics.[5]

If you are giving less than a tithe, take a hard look at the reasons why. The most likely reasons are lack of faith or holding on tightly to money. If you receive an average income at something like $60,000 per household, a tithe would be $6000 or $500 a month. The average giving by Christians of all denominations is around 5% to all causes. That would mean you are probably already giving $250 per month.

I assume here that you desire to gain access to the best results that God can offer you. Even if your aspirations are lower, you may find that tithing blesses your life. Still, if you do want all that God has planned for you, the question becomes: how can you be prepared to go wherever God calls you? Can you possibly walk away from your earthly possessions, if you are still so attached to your possessions that you think you cannot give God the balance of his tithe?

The amazing thing about tithing and faith and doing what God wants you to do is that the ultimate results of your choices will bring you more "wealth." The wealth God builds for you may not be tangible. Spiritual wealth is not about things you can touch. The wealth God gives you produces joy, and nobody can steal it.

Sacrificing because you love God

Since you are a Christian, you cannot possibly be stingy, greedy, or grasping. In fact, you would be quick to dive into a cold lake to save your child, risking your own life to save theirs. When you were dating, your poems spoke of crawling across hot embers in order to be by her side. If there were not enough food to go around, your kids would get the most, while you would suffer in silence. We all wish to be that heroic, but are we?

A Little Test

You are in the middle of a great movie, and you're coming to the best part. Your spouse leans over and says, "I'm so sorry, but I just don't feel well. Would it be okay to leave now?" You say what?

Everyone loves Moose Tracks ice cream in your house. There is only barely enough left for one person, and you're standing in front of the freezer staring at the container. You proceed to do what?

It's your spouse's turn to (fill in the blank), but he, or she, is looking really harried, depressed, exhausted. You do what?

A bigger test

Your spouse, sibling, mother, or child has done something very destructive, directly affecting you, your spouse, your kids, and your parents. The guilty party has sincerely asked for forgiveness and now needs your help. Not a little help. Substantial help that you would gladly have given prior to the destructive behavior. Your response?

Okay. Let's make it a God thing. As I have been thinking about what complete surrender means, it occurs to me that my youngest son will soon be a senior in high school. . A senior, with events and trips and graduation, and much more. If God calls me to foreign missions or to move to another state, and if the opportunity is now, not a year from now, how do I respond?

A crazed killer walks into a room where you are in

attendance, and screams at the crowd: "Raise your hand if you are a Christian." Before you say what you would do, think about times when were in a group situation where you should have stood up for God, Christ, the Bible, or the church, but you kept your mouth shut for fear of being seen as radical or weird or not one of the crowd. What will you do?

True love is sacrificial. Is our faith strong enough to make real sacrifices, and/or tiny sacrifices all the time? Cheerfully?

FAST BECAUSE GOD IS MOST IMPORTANT

Jesus told His disciples that some things only come out by prayer and fasting. (See Mark 9:29) In Matt 6:16 He said "When you fast . . . ." Not if you fast. Yet many Christians think that fasting isn't important.

Dr. Bill Bright has been motivating me for years. His dedication to God is an example everyone can admire. Dr. Bright started a movement for fasting, in which he led entire churches in 40-day fasts. He also wrote at least four books on fasting which you may find on Amazon or at other booksellers. So if my words inspire you to fast, you might want to read one of those four books or at least refer to his free online short course.

I have only fasted three times for more than a day. Each time I felt that I was being called to fast and that I needed to deal with issues that required more than prayer as mentioned in Mark 9:29. Each of those times of fasting was very beneficial in my faith walk, in my closeness to God, and in working through the issues. It was easy to stay motivated during the physically roughest moments (the afternoon of the 2nd day), because I was very clear about my motives and the benefits.

A fourth time I started a three-day fast, but I did not have those elements lined up. I was not clear that God was calling me to do it. I was not clear on what the purpose was. I became very weak and headachy on the 2nd day, and ended the fast.

Most who write on the subject refer to four types of fasts and two methods. The time of fasting might be one full day. Some will eat a last meal at dinner, then not eat again until dinner the next day. Essentially this method skips two meals. I consider this as a good way to practice fasting, but I find it hard to imagine that it is very useful in either the sacrificial aspect or in the extra time allotted to visiting with God.

A one-day fast might be more useful if there were three meals missed. This might mean that the time of the fast was more than 24 hours, but I believe it would be much more meaningful. The greater sacrifice of time and nutrition would allow for greater focus. Frankly, even a three meal fast is not difficult.

Three-day fasts are difficult, and those who have fasted for much longer times usually say that the 2nd day is still the hardest. Giving over at least three days of time, concentrated attention, and sacrificing meals is something you should be praying about doing. Unlike the other disciplines, I see nothing in the Bible to suggest that this should be a weekly or monthly or quarterly event in your life.

It is a great preview to the final chapter in this work. When you are prepared, and when you are called, and when you have clarity, act. Obey. Go.

Daniel inspired the 21-day fast. Jesus and others completed 40-day fasts. During shorter fasts, you might allow yourself only water. During longer fasts, you will probably need to allow for juices and/or broth. Longer fasts of this type should be done only after a doctor's approval and with help and encouragement from your wise counselors.

In summary, I would counsel you to make yourself available to fast as God calls you or as the Holy Spirit leads you. In particular, when facing a particularly difficult situation where prayer may seem to be not enough, fasting is clearly called for. This might include you own failure of faith in any of the areas of discipline already outlined, your own inability to deal with any ongoing sin, or your own failure to move forward to accept a clear call from God.

FORGIVE BECAUSE YOU ARE FORGIVEN

There are several themes that form the central tenets of the Bible: Love, redemption, justice, grace, good and evil, and of course, forgiveness. God establishes the principle of forgiveness by modeling it often in His own actions, then making it a core principle of Jesus' teaching for his followers.

God, through Jesus, placed a very high value on forgiveness. When we say the Lord's Prayer, we stop with Matt 6:13. Maybe people should also pray the next two verses:

For if you forgive other people when they sin against you, your heavenly Father will also forgive you. But if you do not forgive others their sins, your Father will not forgive your sins. Matthew 6:14-15

From this verse it would appear obvious that God wanted to make absolutely clear the importance of forgiveness. Certainly the theme is picked up again and again throughout the New Testament, and the same intensity can be seen in the parable of the unforgiving servant.

Therefore, the kingdom of heaven is like a king who wanted to settle accounts with his servants. As he began the settlement, a man who owed him ten thousand bags of gold was brought to him. Since he was not able to pay, the master ordered that he and his wife and his children and all that he had be sold to repay the debt.

"At this the servant fell on his knees before him. 'Be patient with me,' he begged, 'and I will pay back everything.' The servant's master took pity on him, canceled the debt and let him go.

But when that servant went out, he found one of his fellow servants who owed him a hundred silver coins. He grabbed him and began to choke him. 'Pay back what you owe me!' he demanded.

His fellow servant fell to his knees and begged him, 'Be patient with me, and I will pay it back.'

But he refused. Instead, he went off and had the man thrown into prison until he could pay the debt. When the other servants saw what had happened, they were outraged and went and told their master everything that had happened.

Then the master called the servant in. 'You wicked servant,' he said, 'I canceled all that debt of yours because you begged me to. Shouldn't you have had mercy on your fellow servant just as I had on you?' In anger his master handed him over to the jailers to be tortured, until he should pay back all he owed.

This is how my heavenly Father will treat each of you unless you forgive your brother or sister from your heart.

Matthew 18:23-35

If you are having issues with an inability to forgive it may stem from three sources. For most, it is a failure to forgive someone else for pain or injustice received. Another large group is unable to forgive themselves for pain or injustice they have inflicted on others. Then yet another group blames God for pain or injustice; they struggle to forgive God for this perceived trespass.

Failure to forgive leads to other sins, such as bitterness and anger, which give rise to retribution, verbal or physical assault, and even murder. When we are unable to forgive after experiencing a wrong, the emotional wound festers, becoming like an infection that destroys both body and spirit. If not controlled, and the only real control is to forgive, then those who cannot forgive open themselves to demonic influence.

Everyone has at some time suffered the inability to forgive. Whether an individual is unable to forgive others, himself, or

God, it is sin. For the purposes of this chapter I will concentrate on the one that seems to be uppermost in God's concern: failure to forgive others.

Notice that I am writing about forgiveness under the heading of discipline. In the course of our daily lives we constantly negotiate relationship issues with family, friends, neighbors, co-workers, bosses, employees, government, and church brothers and sisters. The opportunity for real or imagined hurt is always a mere conversation away. Therefore, the daily consideration of whether we need to forgive someone seems to be as important as any other discipline.

There are four reasons why it makes no sense to continue to carry around anger and bitterness towards another person, even when their "crime" against you has been horrific, and even when they have made no effort to say they are sorry or ask for forgiveness:

1. Because God told you to. That should be enough on the subject. However, God goes further to point out that He has forgiven you at least as much.
2. Because it does not hurt the person that you fail to forgive. It is only hurting you, emotionally, and often physically.
3. Because your failure to forgive will have no effect on how or when the other person is punished.
4. Because God does not tell you that you must reconcile with the person, only that you need to forgive. God forgets the forgiven sin. He does not so instruct us. There are, in fact, people whom we must forgive with whom it would be dangerous to reconcile.

How do you know when you are done with an issue of forgiveness? Sometimes we say that we forgive someone, and yet we still feel that knot in the stomach or neck when we think of them or the event that caused the trespass. Here are three ways to test yourself.

1. You no longer want anything bad to happen to the person
2. You only wish them the best
3. You pray for them! Remember that God has instructed us to pray for our enemies.

Can you hear from God while you are still harboring anger? I heard from God when I was definitely carrying a small bitter pill against one person. However, as noted above, there are degrees of failure to forgive. If your attitude is interfering with your walk and causing you to act out on your resentments, then it is unlikely that you will be of much use to God until it is resolved.

If you believe that you have a major issue with forgiveness, I recommend the book *The Bondage Breaker*, by Neil Anderson. Of the many books I've read on the subject, he has provided the best and most succinct formula for overcoming resistance to forgiving.

Chapter 7—Be Vulnerable

Like a Child

I'm not 100% certain that there is a clear line between the disciplines just covered and this next group of actions which give evidence that you are walking closely with God:

- Praising
- Asking
- Repenting

In my personal walk and in conversations with others about their spiritual life, I have concluded that people are confused about praising, asking, and repenting. Christian friends tell me that sometimes one practice is easy while another is hard. The challenges of each day prevent any sense of consistency in the ability to do these things every day.

For me, it is generally easy to praise, difficult to ask, and very hard to repent. More recently it is easier to ask, I commonly forget to praise, and I rarely get around to repenting. Does any of this sound like you?

Christians must remember that God does not need our praises, gains nothing from our requests, and loves us before we repent. Therefore, praising, asking, and repenting are for us. They help us grow spiritually, gain greater humility, and draw closer to God. The premise of this entire book is that as we grow closer to God, we will be more likely to hear and respond to His calling, and will be more prepared to do what he asks us to do.

PRAISE—ADORATION AND THANKFULNESS

Praise is easy for me. I could easily beat the drum so loudly that your ears would hurt. I am an optimist with no genetic ability to be depressed or even negative for long. This is not always a wonderful set of attributes, especially since it makes it hard for me to empathize with those who are inclined towards being negative, depressed, anxious, or worried.

When I see roses, I don't see thorns. This is a problem if you need to tend the rose bush. You can get hurt. Those in my camp are said to see the world through rose colored glasses, and this can mean being out of touch with reality.

The good news is that the Bible endorses optimism as a lifestyle, while noting we need to count the cost, which should rein in my type. Obviously, my personality type will find it easier to praise, because everything appears good enough all the time.

The Bible calls on us to praise God for His blessings (Psalm 100 among many), and even to praise Him for our troubles (Rom 5: 3-5). Why would this be? First and foremost praising someone else for your blessings is an act of humility. There are many instances in the Bible where God deals harshly with those who believe that they have achieved great things or gained success by their own devices. The Old Testament makes an example of Nebuchadnezzar, who looked over all that he had done and got all puffed up about it. He spent the next seven years crazed and acting like an animal, even eating grass.

God creates us, provides everything, and offers us many gifts including the potential for eternal life with Him. Praise for those blessing would be a start, but there is much more.

Most of us in the Western World enjoy luxuries that kings could not imagine as recently as 100 years ago. So praising God for our normal day-in-and-day-out food, clothing, housing, transportation, choices of entertainment, travel, and careers should be easy to add to things like life, health, air, and basics. Sure, it might be easy to complain about any of these things, too. In my house we currently use an aged 700-watt microwave. It takes 2 minutes to warm up what should only take 90 seconds on a newer model. To hear the kids talk, you would think we were cooking our food over hot rocks carried from an underground steam vent. Praise Him for what we have.

Most of us have some or even many relationships that are worthy of praise: parents, siblings, children, spouses, grandkids, other relatives, friends, coworkers, as well as brothers and sisters in the Lord who bless our lives. If you are like me, some of these folks are currently causing you pain, frustration, or even worse. However, many are also blessing your socks off.

Our lives are easy. We work fewer years, fewer hours per day, fewer days per week, at less menial tasks than any generation in history. The ease with which we prepare our foods, wash our clothes, deal with waste, and maintain our homes and yards leaves us with an amazing amount of free time, or at least time that is ours to manage. And yet I read an article just yesterday that said over 50% of us hate our jobs or are just going through the motions.

I fear that for some today it is necessary to point out how amazing it is to be living in freedom, with relative peace and security. For some today, all of the above seems so normal that there has grown up a sense of entitlement. Praising God for all of these things damps down that idea of entitlement, which is corrosive to our lives, and retards our ambitions.

When a nation or even the entire world fails to thank the Creator, we become a society that believes that humans no longer need God. If we can grow human cells in a lab, then use those cells to create an organ which can then replace a diseased organ, we may start to believe that we have reached a point where we the created no longer need the Creator. Rather we should be humble enough to note that God has provided us the gifts that allow for the creative acts.

As for this notion of praising God for in the midst of trouble, even crisis? Paul explained it this way in Romans:

> *Not only so, but we also glory in our sufferings, because we know that suffering produces perseverance; perseverance, character; and character, hope. And hope does not put us to shame, because God's love has been poured out into our hearts through the Holy Spirit, who has been given to us.*
> Rom 5:3-5

There will be suffering, trials, sickness, or accidents in every human life, believer or not. How like God to use these natural circumstances in life to our personal benefit! After we have persevered, we are in a better position to be a blessing to others who are going through similar struggles.

If you have a problem praising, maybe you should make a list. Start with the ideas above. You might add your talents, skills, spiritual gifts, training, community, political leadership (that's a hard one, but we are specifically called to do so), God's discipline, and even your troubles. The last two are also a bit more difficult than praising God for providing the fantastic lunch you are about to consume. The Bible reminds us that a father who doesn't discipline his child doesn't love that child. Troubles are designed to add character and wisdom.

One last bit about praise. The Bible also shows Paul and others taking credit for things. The fact that God wants us to praise Him for everything in no way means that we are not responsible for our good choices and our good works. I appreciate the athlete that says he gives God all the glory. I would appreciate his statement more if he said that he has worked his rear end off for twenty years and is thankful to God for being a part of the process and allowing him to reach this place. False humility that doesn't take into consideration human effort is not the answer. Giving God all the glory for His part in the process is what this author humbly believes we are called to do.

Ask and receive

Here comes my biggest confession of all. I am "the Beave." I was a towhead, blue eyed, bright, smiling kid who grew up under Truman, Eisenhower, and Kennedy. We cured polio, were the greatest nation on earth, and decided to send a man to the moon.

My personal life was also inordinately blessed. No major crises until my 30s. I enjoyed plenty of love, family, solid direction, and Christ at the center. There was also an underlying theme of the time that was a big part of who I was and am. "You can be anything you want to be. You can be President of the United States. You can … you can … you can!" I believed it and I lived it. I won't bore you with the details. You can find it all online. The fact that I'm writing on this subject, and believe that I have the ability to write a book or something important enough to say comes from that upbringing.

The result for me, and many like me who grew up in that era, is that I really do believe I can do anything. If I believe that idea, why do I need anyone else, even God, to help? There are plenty of Christians in every era, all over the world, who believe it.

If I don't need any help to get what I need or want, why would I pray for God's help? Why would God care whether I ask for His help, if I'm praising Him daily for all that He has provided and earnestly giving Him credit?

It is easy for some believers to ask God for help. They request that their needs be filled. They intercede for others. Some ask for their wants. They feel comfortable asking God for a new Mercedes Benz or a trip to the French Riviera.

This group is quick to point to the cantankerous widow in the Biblical parable who kept bugging the judge every day for her rights, until he simply wearied of hearing about it. Some even take it to the extreme of whining, complaining, or showing anger because, "I did not receive what I asked for, and I want it now." They forget that God's answer to prayer may not be wish fulfillment. He might defer the request or deny it altogether.

Why does God want us to ask Him for things? How are we to ask? What are we to expect? Is it enough to know that God's answer will be "Yes," "no," "maybe later" or some form of better understanding, insight, or discernment?

Let's examine these three issues in order.

Why does God want us to ask Him for things?

1. God wants to bless us. Over and over throughout the scriptures God makes it clear that He wants to fill our needs, bless us, expand our territory, provide for us, and make our life on earth as joyful as possible. While He knows exactly what we need and want, He also knows what He will give us if we ask.

God wants us to act on our faith.

He replied, "Because you have so little faith. Truly I tell you, if you have faith as small as a mustard seed, you can say to this mountain, 'Move from here to there,' and it will move. Nothing will be impossible for you."

Matthew 17:20-21

God Called

Therefore I tell you, whatever you ask for in prayer, believe that you have received it, and it will be yours.

Mark 11:24

Many of Jesus' healings took place after someone asked, and he often commented on the faith of the person asking. He also criticized some for not having enough faith. When we have the kind of faith that the Apostles had, we will be capable of doing anything they did and more. God wants us to act on our faith and discover what he does in response.

1. God wants us to learn humility. It cannot be overemphasized that when we think we can do it all, we have no reason to ask. For most of us, it is not intuitive to go to God for direction. I notice that sometimes even when I'm particularly trusting God for the solution, I still try to take back the control. All too frequently we have to dig ourselves a really deep hole before we ask Him for a rope.
2. God wants us to understand Him better. One of the benefits of keeping a prayer journal is that we can keep track of our prayer requests and the eventual answers. As we see how God acts in response to our prayers, we gain greater understanding of how He works. If we pay attention, we might find that we become "better" at praying in ways that are more likely to line up with God's intentions.
3. God wants us to have good testimonies. As we pray and receive answers, we are able to deepen our own belief. Therefore the answers themselves provide a testimony to the one praying. Then we are able to tell others about our experience and it becomes a testimony of God's grace, mercy, power, and goodness.
4. God wants us to see the way He works. In the Old

Testament, God often laid hard tasks on chosen individuals in order that the nations would understand that He was God. When we lack faith, our limited prayers limit what God can do for us. God wants us to have faith that is willing to ask God to do things that clearly testify to His power.

HOW ARE WE TO ASK?

- Pray in Jesus' name. "Ask anything in my name." Simple enough. I commonly forget. I tack "in Jesus precious name I pray," to the end of any public prayer, but truly, it is not always earnestly considered. If we were to think about the reality of asking for the result in His name, it should cause us to pause and reflect on the significance of that act. Can we still ask for something frivolous or out of step with His will if we have carefully added on "in Jesus name?"
- Pray, "If it be your will." When Jesus prayed to His Father on the night before his crucifixion, he made a request, but he then said, "If it be your will." Once again this approach should bring us to a more sober assessment of our prayer. Everything we pray should be lined up with God's will. Making this statement a part of our requests should help us to keep that in front of mind.
- Pray expecting an answer. Have you ever prayed, "Lord, I really need to stop being mean to my co-worker," and then listened attentively for God to show the way? Remember, He may give you the answer through Scripture (assuming you are reading any), wise counsel (assuming you are seeking any), or circumstances (assuming you are open to applying them). The important thing is to remember that when we pray and

request something, God wants us to expect an answer. We should ask for:

- Wisdom
- Spiritual gifts such as faith, leadership, teaching, encouraging
- Fruit of the Spirit such as love, joy, peace, patience
- The needs of others
- Kingdom things such as peace on earth, restoration of our land, the spread of the gospel
- Greater faith, opportunities to witness, righteousness
- Removal of the Devil and his demons from people or places

The list could be very long. These are some notable examples that may inspire greater faith to ask God for many things.

Of course these are the kinds of things that God most wants you to request. Should you ask for a new car, a better microwave, a win for the home team, or a boyfriend? Sure. God wants to bless you, but I love this saying: God is not just a big vending machine in the sky. Be attentive to God's guidance as you pray for such things.

What are we to expect in response to our prayers?

We are guaranteed that God will provide what we need. We can also find scriptures that promise us wisdom if we pray and ask for it. Not all wisdom, certainly, but wisdom. In fact, if you go back over the list just above, we are promised most of those things if we ask. We are not promised every spiritual gift, but we will be provided with one or more. The kingdom items will not show up immediately or for everyone. Our intercessory prayers may be answered with a "no."

We are not promised that we will be provided with our wants, but God does teach us to ask. There are also things we might ask for that are unselfish and beneficial to the kingdom, but are not promised. We might pray to be a soloist on the praise team. We might desire to help in children's ministry. These requests are all subject to three oft-repeated options: Yes, no, and maybe later, not to mention more complex answers.

We may be provided with greater understanding, insight, or discernment as a result of our request. God may show us why the request was not appropriate, or timely, or that it might have even been harmful.

An example of the latter might be asking for financial wealth. For many people having wealth would be a curse. God clearly shows us that many will turn material possessions or wealth into an idol, a reason for worry, or a source of pride, division, or even mayhem.

There are many reasons to ask God for his help and provision. Sometimes sin keeps us from asking. Remember that asking is one way we poise ourselves to hear the voice of God with a clear call to action.

Repentance

When was the last time you repented? To be clearer, when was the last time you sincerely repented of a specific sin, crying out to God that you know just how much your sin hurt Him, and asking for His help in turning from that sin and towards holiness?

Can you even recall the last time you did any such thing? You may have recited the Lord's Prayer asking God to forgive your trespasses. Did you contemplate even for a few seconds, any specific sin. Were you able to remember any sin you had committed?

Why is it so hard for us to be repentant? Here are a few reasons we might recognize:

1) I can't think of any sin I've committed.
2) I don't want to repent of the sins I can think of.
3) There are some minor sins, but surely God isn't interested in the pencils I copped from the office.
4) I have so many prayer requests and other things to cover in my devotion time that I simply skip the repenting part.
5) I can't go there, because it is too painful to think about, much less tell God about.

If you have read through the preceding tough chapters, and if you are still excited about where this all leads, you could almost be compared to the disciples who stayed with Jesus after others complained that Jesus' teaching was too hard.

If you have taken the preceding material to heart and if you have begun to practice some of these disciplines, you should be ready for what comes next. Please do not let your arrival at this point lead to pride. You are here because the Holy Spirit is leading your willing heart.

We can rejoice when we are maturing, but there is no place for pride. Remember the questions for self-examination that leads to repentance. ***If we are not repenting we are not following God's commands.*** If we are not repenting on a continuous basis, we leave ourselves open for attacks from the Devil, and we are not understanding the heart of God. Paul understood the need to be continuously repenting:

> *So I find this law at work:*
> *Although I want to do good, evil is right there with me. For in my inner being I delight in God's law; but I see another law at work in me, waging war against the law of my mind and making me a prisoner of the law of sin at work within me. 24 What a wretched man I am! Who will rescue me from this body that is subject to death? Thanks be to God, who delivers me through Jesus Christ our Lord!*

So then, I myself in my mind am a slave to God's law, but in my sinful nature a slave to the law of sin.

Romans 7:21-25

In preparation for this chapter, I went in search of solid teaching on repentance. I recommend *Repentance:* The First Word of the Gospel by Richard Owen Roberts, with a foreword by Henry Blackaby. This book led me to deep repentance. I first repented of my failure to repent. Then I repented of pride, unbelief, and lack of faith.

Everyone suffers the blindness that results in a failure to recognize the need for repentance. Some of the things that break God's heart don't make much impact on our hearts. We think some of our sins are more significant than others. God does not rank sins. God's heart is broken when you:

- Call someone a fool
- Are angry without a righteous reason
- Gossip (Lest you excuse yourself from this behavior, you need to think about the definition. Gossip is speaking about another in a way that may cause them harm, even if that harm is only to diminish them in the view of those listening. When you speak about someone in a hurtful way with the intent of building yourself up you are gossiping.)
- Lie, exaggerate, cut corners, cheat (e.g. tests, insurance claims, taxes) and the like
- Fail to forgive
- Lust after another (It could be porn or imagining yourself with someone who is not your spouse.)
- Have sex outside of marriage. (If you think it is sex, it is.)

- Intentionally inflict pain on another, whether physical or emotional

Take a few quiet moments and be honest with God about these things.

THE BIG THREE - PRIDE, UNBELIEF, LACK OF FAITH

After we acknowledge our need to repent, we need to face the pride that kept us blind to that need. When we humble our pride, we are able to see how our failure to trust God stymied our willingness to repent. Finally, we discover how lack of faith was always at the root of the sense that we were doing pretty well, and we hardly had anything to repent of.

To help illustrate our sin in each of these areas, I will use the example of giving. For many Christians, giving to God is a very touchy subject. Answer the 20 questions below honestly:

1. Are you giving because you think it will provide future treasure in heaven?
2. Are you giving so that you will be blessed?
3. Are you giving because you feel pressured?
4. Do you carefully analyze the amount?
5. Have you ever hoped that someone else would notice how much you are giving?
6. Have you worried that others will notice how little you are giving?
7. Have you noticed how much or little others are giving?
8. Have you wondered or cared how much you give compared to others?
9. Do you always give cheerfully or sometimes begrudge the amount?
10. Have you concerned yourself that the funds you are giving may not be used as you think they should be?

11. Have you failed to honor a pledge, whether pledged publicly or just to God?
12. Have you ever given even one dime sacrificially? Think about that. What does sacrificial giving mean to you?
13. Have you ignored an opportunity to help someone even though you believed God was prompting you to meet that need?
14. Do you tithe?
15. If you don't tithe, why not?
16. Do you feel that God doesn't need the money?
17. Is it equally clear that the church, pastor, etc., are not counting on your money (or shouldn't be)? In other words, do you believe that God's work is not going to be put on hold if you fail to give?
18. Do you give as an act of worship and obedience, and as a blessing to others?
19. If the pastor said from the pulpit this Sunday that the church had more money than it knew what to do with, would you give the same amount anyway?
20. Do you cringe when the pastor or elders ask for greater giving?

Now apply the same thinking to your attitudes and intentions regarding your spouse, kids, parents, neighbors, boss, employees, friends, possessions, community, country, and fellow believers.

In other words, your mind (and mine) is almost always on yourself, your needs, your wants, and your desires. Your motives include the desire to be liked, respected, appreciated, and approved. You want more stuff, better entertainment, longer life, and greater beauty. You parent in ways that reduce your pain or inconvenience, increase your personal standing in your

God Called

community, and "make you proud." You want to change your spouse to meet your own desires, or you want your spouse to remain unchanged by life experience. You want your husband or wife to meet your needs and make you look good. You are angry when your expectations are not met.

Your goal in life should be doing God's will, worshiping Him, and growing in relationship with Him. In order to do those things you must die to yourself. You must stop majoring on you. Repent of your focus on pleasing self. Change your mind, and focus on pleasing God. Choose to bless others in what you do, what you think, and what you prioritize.

The primary reason for such self-interest is that you do not trust God or the Scriptures. You don't fully believe God or the Bible. This may be due in part to your experience. You see that godly people still face calamities. You may feel that you are a good soldier, moving mountains for God, telling others about Jesus, and getting callouses on your knees, only to experience some great loss or even several great losses. Experience weakens your belief. Your faith is diminished. You are less joyful about giving. Your ministry becomes a joyless volunteer job. Faith is weighed down and overwhelmed when self feels wounded, because self-interest trumps faith in God.

"Repent!" said John the Baptist.

In those days John the Baptist came, preaching in the wilderness of Judea and saying, "Repent, for the kingdom of heaven has come near." This is he who was spoken of through the prophet Isaiah.
Matthew 3:1-3

From that time on Jesus began to preach, "Repent, for the kingdom of heaven has come near."
Matthew 4:17

These are the first words of John and Jesus in the gospel. Repent of your unbelief.

Contemporary people need to repent just like the people John the Baptist reproached. Will we repent for the right reason—because we love God and know that our failure to repent has broken His heart?

Feature Story—Sin Gets in the Way

Model of Jerusalem at the time of Christ.

Earlier in the book, I shared a story of having received a call from God during prayer time. The story that follows does not come to a positive ending, but you can see God at every turn.

The Bible that says that if we are faithful in small things God will give us more things to handle for Him. Many years after the "Sex Kills" book, I had a vision, like a daydream, an image laid out in great detail. Like before, the vision came at a time when I had made myself available to God to use as He pleased. It did not happen because I am special, but rather because I was immersed and disciplined, and I fervently desired to be used by God to accomplish His mission.

THE VISION

As with the previous book, God laid out a clear vision of creating a Christian theme park that became a book length description of the park. It was to be the quality of a Disney park. The primary design was a place where guests would discover the Bible by encountering it in the 21st Century environment.

The park would have at its center, a full-sized model of Jerusalem at the time of Christ.

As if to confirm the fact that the vision was from God, the next morning over breakfast I saw a feature article in the *Los Angeles Times* about the design of theme park rides that forecast designs for rides of the future. The story included interviews with major designers and mentions of the very kinds of companies I would need to create the park.

I can assure you that I was serious about this. In fact, I put together a board of directors made up of successful business owners who were all committed, mature Christians. The board met and began the process of making decisions to move forward. In addition to the board, I met with my pastor and other "wise counselors" to explain the vision and to confirm that the idea was indeed a vision.

One of the people I called was a very dear friend who was a fount of knowledge and understanding about Biblical history and the designs of historical buildings, art, and treasure. He was an artist who had designed replicas of historic buildings.

As I told him about my vision, he listened in silence. He had a relative who was trying to raise funds for a similar effort, a project that would ultimately include my friend in the design of the theme park. You may believe in coincidences. I don't. This only further cemented my conviction that the source of the idea was God.

As I look back on this time, I recall that I was as excited about these developments as I could possibly be. My life circumstances were not perfect. They never are. Nevertheless, they don't get much better than this period in my life.

The Fall

Dreamstime.com

Today I am not sure which of the following events were causes and which were consequences. My best guess is that my company's financial condition, and my sinful response to it undermined this project and a whole lot more. The details are not necessary here, but I engaged in business practices that were extremely inappropriate in order to keep the company going. I hurt several people who were witnesses to my behavior and others whom I asked to cover my tracks.

The situation was triggered when, at the worst possible moment, the landlord asked us to move from our business location after eighteen years. They had decided that they wanted a different kind of business in the location. Our business was light manufacturing; they wanted a distribution business such as import/export or wholesale.

We made the move, but it was a disaster. The cost of the move put us deeper in the hole. Immediately after the move, the new building was hit by lightning. We had been forced out of a good location, our new location was severely damaged, and things did not look good.

We put the business up for sale. Then I was caught in my transgression.

As soon as I recognized my behavior for sin, I quietly stopped working on the theme park project. I believed that maybe the problem would be solved quickly. I could face God, and then try to pick up the pieces and continue. I couldn't. I stopped all efforts on the project in 2006.

I am thankful that the person most affected by my sin was very kind and forgiving and is still a close friend today. Yet the consequence of sin was the undoing of the project to which God had called me.

Looking back, divine involvement seemed quite clear in both the *Sex Kills* book project and the theme park project. In both cases there are dozens of people who know everything that took place and can confirm those events detail for detail. However, in one case, the book *Sex Kills*, I answered the call and moved forward, even if I did stumble here and there. In the case of the theme park, I answered the call, but the world tripped me up. I allowed myself to fall to a level I never previously thought possible.

Chapter 8—Listen at All Times

God speaks to us through His creation

Communication is an amazing thing. We communicate with one another in many ways. Even before we are born we start learning to communicate. We can be driven out of our minds when deprived of communication. Yet we often fail miserably in our attempts to communicate with one another.

Sadly, our experience is the same in our communication with God. Most of us are very poor at this critical skill, even though God has created an arsenal of ways that He can communicate His desires for our lives. We almost seem to go out of our way to ignore Him, misunderstand Him, and confuse His voice with that of the Devil. Many Christians are quite capable of talking to God, but they find it extremely difficult to listen for His answers, statements, and direction.

If you want to hear from God, you need to hear His passionate plea in Isaiah 6:9 as quoted by Jesus in Mark:

When he was alone, the Twelve and the others around him asked him about the parables. He told them, "The secret of the kingdom of God has been given to you. But to those on the outside everything is said in parables so that, 'they may be ever seeing but never perceiving, and ever hearing but never understanding; otherwise they might turn and be forgiven!'"

Mark 4:10-12

This quotation appears multiple times throughout the Old and New Testament. (Isaiah 6:9; Mark 4:12; Matt 13:14; Luke 8:10; Acts 28: 27; Romans 11:8) This statement tells us that the reason we do not comprehend the message we are well able to see and hear is the deafness of our hearts.

You have seen this happen with children. Think of an 8 year-old who is told how to do something he clearly doesn't want to do. His eyes are rolling, his face is blank, and his body is slumping. If anyone asks him what was just said, he cannot express it, unless maybe to parrot back the exact remark. Despite all the evidence that this child can hear what is being said, it is quite evident that it is not penetrating his unwillingness to learn.

We might also compare our level of awareness to our observation, or lack of it, in our everyday world. We drive down a residential street in a two-ton vehicle capable of inflicting massive damage on living creatures. We could be carefully scanning the entire space in front of us, keeping our full wits about us, checking rear view mirrors constantly, and keeping an ear out for warning signals such as screeching breaks, shouts, or warnings from inside the car. Instead the radio is blaring, cell phones are handy, conversations are in process, and hot coffee is being consumed.

If we were attentive, we would see and hear God's efforts to communicate with us every day. We ignore some of God's messages because we don't think the communication channel he uses is sufficiently godly.

We may try to limit the ways God can communicate with us, but God does not limit our freedom to communicate with him. In the Bible, God teaches us many ways to communicate with him. Here is a sampling of the many ways God communicates His guidance and directions to us:

SCRIPTURE

Most Christians agree that God's primary method of communicating with us is through the Bible. Most Christian leaders and teachers agree that we should test any communication that we believe to be from God against the guidance of Scripture. Secular thinkers believe that human beings have outgrown the ancient Scriptures, but Christians know that the truth of Scripture does not change.

If we are consistently reading the Bible, and if we open our ears and heart to what is being said, we will hear from God. He promises that the Holy Spirit is teaching us as we read.

HOLY SPIRIT NUDGING AND GUIDING

And your ears shall hear a word behind you, saying:

"This is the way, walk in it," when you turn to the right or when you turn to the left."

Isaiah 30:21

The guidance of the Holy Spirit is very important. The Spirit works through Scripture, and Scripture confirms the guidance of the Spirit.

The most frequent nudging we are likely to receive is to "shut up." Our failure to put a governor on our tongue is likely the greatest source of sins, both commission and omission. How often do we willfully "fail to hear" the Holy Spirit reminding us not to say what does not need to be said?

We are also prone not to hear the nudging when called to acts of kindness, giving, discipline (of ourselves or those under our charge), and forgiving or asking forgiveness. Many times when we hear or feel the Holy Spirit nudge us, we recall Scripture that either does or does not support our belief of being nudged. It is not an accident that we remember those verses at that time.

OTHER PEOPLE

Often we hear the word of God in the words of others. They may be teachers, prophets, counselors, parents, friends or even people we meet by chance. Unfortunately, we can also hear plenty of advice or direction that is unscriptural, even from pastors. Pastors, prophets, teachers, and others who mean well can easily cherry-pick Scripture out of context or completely misconstrue God's intent. We are not obligated to follow even the most devout Christian; we are obligated to follow God. The Bereans had it right. Test everything against the Bible. Test even when the writer or the speaker has quoted Scripture in support of their teaching or advice.

WITNESS OF OTHERS

Have you ever read *The Book of Martyrs* or anything written by Corrie Ten Boom or Charles Colson? Such stories often encourage me and motivate me to become more effective in producing fruit.

God can speak to us in many ways through their lives, just as He did with stories of the various personalities in the Bible. Common men and women perform unbelievable deeds of courage. Those same heroes also do very stupid things and sin in ways that we cannot comprehend.

The witness of others can help us understand God's intentions for our lives in unlimited ways. How should we act? How are we likely to act? How do we recover from our sins? Whom can we emulate? Whom should we be careful to avoid? It is possible that someone we meet by the most inexplicable chance is someone God has placed in our path to share something we need at that moment.

Circumstances—Open and Closed Doors

Jesus, and later Paul, made many observations and gave directions regarding how to *read* circumstances, for example when spreading the word. Jesus said that if a town rejected the gospel, it was appropriate to leave and go where the response was better. The disciples were to "dust off their feet" as they left town. We often call such situations examples of closed doors.

Jesus used circumstances as opportunities to teach. Examples are many: the woman at the well, the centurion whose daughter was sick, or His encounters with those who sought Him for healing. He understood that the circumstances offered the potential for helping someone in need, and also for explaining a kingdom principle to His followers. These would be examples of open doors.

Nature and Creation

Jesus used nature as examples throughout Scripture. When we meditate on creation and the amazing things God has created, we often find inspiration that helps us to understand God and to get clarity about His purposes.

God says that only a fool will look at nature and not see Him. The more we learn about how things work, the more clearly we see that none of this could happen without God. However, God doesn't stop at creation. The rules of nature must be enforced, and the forces of nature must be renewed.

One has to wonder why an atheist isn't shocked every time an object is dropped and falls on the floor instead of the ceiling. One can just as easily wonder at a believer who sees that the birds are fed and the flowers clothed through no effort of their own, and yet doubt God's ability to do the same for people.

Discipline

The opening chapters of this book covered many different types of Christian discipline. Each one represents an ongoing conversation between you and God. The very acts involved in each discipline require that you consider Him as you participate in the discipline. You cannot give, pray, read your Bible, worship, fast, serve, or sincerely and deeply forgive without thinking of God. Yet it is possible to ignore His direction even when you are practicing these disciplines. You can think about God intellectually and ignore him spiritually at the same time. You must decide to be open and available to hear from Him and to follow.

Answered prayer—ours and others

What is common in your communication with almost everyone in your life? You proceed based on how they respond to you! When you specifically reach out to another with praise, forgiveness, repentance, happiness, anger, requests, or simple fellowship, you are entering into communication. You expect a response. It is exactly the same with God, and he has promised you a response to your prayers. His responses are often far more detailed and complex than yes, no, or maybe later. God is not limited by our imagination of the possibilities. There will be answers to everything you ask.

We also hear from God through the answered prayers of others. We see God working in the lives of other people, and we hear them testify to His blessing in their lives. We also hear stories of disappointment—disappointment in the answer, or disappointment that there seemed to be no answer. Such stories give us the opportunity to be the voice of God in their lives by providing assurance and comfort.

We can meet God in the answers to our prayers and the

prayers of others. We can share answers we receive and thereby encourage others.

Music

I had the opportunity to be part of what may have been the largest choir in history. 1,000,000 men joined to worship and praise God at the Promise Keepers Event in Washington DC. Prior to that I had been carried away by the sound of 80,000 to 100,000 male voices a cappella in various sports stadiums where regional Promise Keepers events were held. The Holy Spirit made Himself felt in our hearts on those occasions through music.

All human beings seek out opportunities to hear music. Most humans feel that it has a spiritual effect on them. The beat, chords, melody, voices, and words that are part of a song inspire, excite, or soothe them. The Bible is filled with songs and with exhortations to sing and play music as forms of praise and worship. The melodies and words of well-known songs and hymns can come back to us just like memorized Scriptures. The association of words and music with spiritual truth makes music a powerful means by which God speaks to us.

Art, Literature, Architecture, and Other Human Endeavors

We can see God's work in nature. *Humans are part of nature.* Therefore we can see God's work and hear His voice through various types of human endeavors. Some of these accomplishments are specifically spiritual. People do not need instruction in the arts to be inspired by the statue of David, the ceiling in Sistine Chapel, or a painting of the Madonna and Child. The works that have been created by Christians in honor of their God are represented in every part of life.

But even human endeavors that are not specifically

intended to give glory to God or show how amazing He is, are, nevertheless, the result of God's gifts. The inventiveness and creativity of humans is a gift of creation, whether or not humans acknowledge it. Human creativity is the image of God manifesting itself in every human being. Thus we might be impressed with Steve Jobs today, but everything he did, including the mental prowess that created the ideas, is from God. We can therefore hear from God in all of what His creatures create.

Fulfilled prophecy

Is your faith faltering? Do you need a faith injection to put you back on track? Study the prophets or read a book on Biblical prophecy. God has spoken thousands of times through dozens of humans who have written down specific statements about what will happen in the future. If even one of these prophetic statements had turned out to be wrong, we might as well throw away the Bible and stop talking about this God of ours.

But none has turned out to be wrong. Moreover, Jesus has specifically fulfilled hundreds of prophecies written to tell of the coming Messiah. Other prophecies written thousands of years ago are clearly coming true today.

Most interesting is the return of the Jews to Israel and Jerusalem after having been scattered for over two centuries. The prophets could not have been more specific about this event that would happen in a future they would never see.

No work of human beings can compare to the Bible. When you see one prophet after another, writing at different times under varying circumstances, but stating the same information about a future event, it speaks to you as loudly as anything else you will ever hear. God is in control. His word is unimpeachable. If we can trust the Bible for its future predictions, we should certainly be able to trust it for daily living.

MIRACLES

In terms of mathematical likelihood and within the limits of human understanding, fulfilled prophecy is a type of miracle. It is not, however, the only type that we recognize. It is the rare Christian who has not received a miraculous intervention or answer to prayer at some time in life. We frequently hear of missionaries rescued by donations from completely unexpected sources, but only after they had spent the last penny of their resources.

We hear about friends with dire, even terminal diagnoses, who return to the doctor to discover that all the indicators of disease and death that had been evident only days before is completely gone. Don't be confused by other cases where the patient dies. We all die. The fact that prayer is answered with a "no" in some cases in no way negates the miracle in another case.

These miracles speak to us of God's power and responsiveness. They help to build up our faith as we see activity on earth that is hard or impossible to explain in scientific terms. They also give evidence of a spiritual realm that may otherwise seem remote and lacking in reality.

DREAMS

God has been speaking to us through dreams since early in the Bible. Jacob's ladder may be one of the most famous dreams, but there are dozens of others. There are those that believe that God no longer speaks to us through dreams. I can find no reason to believe that God isn't using or won't use this method.

On the other hand, my personal opinion is that dreams that carry a message from God will be both infrequent and obvious. I don't believe there is any case in the Bible where the person having the dream didn't know with certainty that God was reaching out through the dream.

Randy Kirk

VISIONS

A vision is similar to a dream except that you are awake. I am convinced that I heard from God through a vision. I had no doubt of it at the time, and I still believe it today. There are many other modern Christians who believe they have had this experience.

Like dreams, visions are infrequent and clearly from God. My experience with a vision was that very specific information was imparted. This would be the case with every Biblical story where someone has a vision.

At the end of the previous chapter is a personal story of having received a vision. It should help you to accept that visions are for today, but it is also told with a twist at the end that carries a second lesson.

ANGELS

Keep on loving one another as brothers and sisters. Do not forget to show hospitality to strangers, for by so doing some people have shown hospitality to angels without knowing it.

Hebrews 13:1-2

Angels exist. They are God's messengers. God still employs angels. I have seen clear evidence of angels acting through human agents to help Christians.

If angels are messengers and deliver messages throughout the Bible, we must be open to the reality that an angel could give us the direction, help, or answer that we are seeking from God. It seems evident that God also uses angels to attract our attention when we are not being faithful or even if we are not saved (for example, Paul on the Damascus Road).

STILL SMALL VOICE

Many mature Christians I know desire to hear from God through a still small voice. Some who claim to have had such an experience (as I do), describe this either as inaudible or almost audible (my experience.) Others say they heard an audible voice. Scripturally, there is a case for both options. On the one hand God made it clear to Elijah (I Kings 19:9-13) that His voice was not in the thunder, earthquake, or fire, but was in fact on a soft breeze. On the other hand, God spoke conversationally with Elijah a few verses later, and with others on many occasions.

As with dreams and visions, you will not have any doubts about such an encounter when it occurs. I was tempted to doubt, because I thought it was completely incredible. My most immediate thought was to confirm that what I heard was actually God speaking in some way outside of my own understanding. (See below)

Too many ways to count

You may have heard this said before—our God is really big. He is capable of doing anything He cares to do within His character. Therefore, as noted in the opening of this chapter, we must be open to hear from God anyway he might choose, rather than hold Him to some preconceived notion. After all, He spoke through Balaam's donkey. If God can use a donkey to speak his message, the possibilities are unlimited.

The message, not the envelope

We should be careful not to yearn for experience over relationship, lest we turn an encounter into an idol. We should all want to hear the voice of God. There are many ways to hear that voice. Most of them do not require any kind of a special *experience*. Therefore, when asking for answers, direction, or wisdom from God, we should not demand that the response come in a certain way. God's word coming from Scripture is every bit as meaningful, important, and useful as His word coming from a burning bush.

It is very easy to become caught up in experiences. We love the feeling of being swept away as part of a large gathering singing or praying together. We are enchanted by a 24-hour prayer vigil. Everyone loves the mountaintop experience after a retreat.

The trap is that we may want a repeat, or an even more amazing experience. The memory of the amazing experience may transcend our memory of God's voice in the experience. Then our desire is no different from any other lust or idol. I speak from experience. Once having heard the still small voice or experienced a vision, I wanted to do that again. Don't allow this type of sinful behavior to interfere with your relationship with Christ.

GOD'S SHEEP KNOW HIS VOICE

We are very near to the end of this journey. The tool chest is almost complete. The basics are all laid out. You now have many tools for hearing and knowing the Shepherd's voice.

On the other hand, if you are not involved in the disciplines and practices outlined thus far, you are in danger of trusting the voice of the deceiver rather than the Redeemer.

You see, the Devil loves nothing better than to fool Christians. He will do anything he can concoct to keep a Christian from being effective. Therefore, he may nudge you, close or open doors, speak through others or give you visions that seem that they could come from God, but are just messed up enough to create chaos. How can you know the difference?

Besides the Devil, you must deal with your own sinful nature. Your mind, working on behalf of your sinful desires may also offer you complete misdirection. Have you heard people express complete peace about what they are doing, when what they are doing is so clearly not of God? How do you know if it is God or your own evil desires?

First, as with anything in life, practice. The more time you spend with God, learning about Him and His ways, the less likely you are to think He is telling you it is okay to steal. Read, pray, listen, obey, observe, start over.

Second, test anything and everything against Scripture. If the Bible says that what you believe to be your direction is not recommended, then the message you think you received is not from God. Are you a Christian who is currently caught up in some sinful activity that is clearly called sin in the Bible? Are you rationalizing that it is fine because your Christian friend said it was? Even if a pastor or elder said it was fine, if the Bible says no, it is not fine.

Third, seek the wise counsel of older and trusted Christian friends; the more the better. If the first one or two that you ask provide an inadequate answer, ask five more.

When a message you think God has spoken does not feel right, seek even more counsel. God does use normal folks for really big works. Still, when you start out on a really big work, you need to be sure you understand the message completely.

Summary

By now you should be actively seeking intimacy with God through the various disciplines outlined in the book to this point. When you are pursuing God with your whole heart, He is almost certainly reaching out to you for your service. In most cases His call will be obvious and easily differentiated from other messages, as it will be scripturally sound. When in doubt, dig deeper into scripture and seek wise counsel.

Chapter 9—Surrender

Abraham surrendered to a clear call from God

This chapter is the reason for the book. This chapter, along with chapter 10 on Holiness, is the end of the journey. Jesus has called us to deny ourselves, take up our own crosses, and follow him. (Matt.16:24-25; Mark 8:34-35; Luke 9:23-24). I believe that most of you are just exactly like me—we give only lip service to this idea.

I have taught on the subject of surrender, discussed surrender with many laymen, discussed the topic on a Christian talk show that I hosted years ago, and interviewed an author whose experience with international ministry led him to write on the subject.

The author made the point that we should be constantly surrendering every aspect of our lives, even the successful parts, because God may have something more, or better, or different for us to do. We may need to be stretched or humbled, or we may need to let go of good work and pass it on to others. Keep in mind that this author was the head of a huge ministry

God Called

that he had founded. I asked him if he had surrendered his own leadership of this ministry to God. Had he told God that he would be prepared to hand it over to others, and go do missionary work in South Los Angeles or start a church?

It was definitely the most telling moment of my three years in talk radio. Dead space on radio is not a good thing, but the featured guest said nothing. He neither denied nor confirmed that he could let go. The silence was the answer.

I had no right to beat him up over his failure to see his own sin. Yet it was clear that his ministry had become an idol. A very fine one with great and noble purposes and achievements, but to him an idol, nevertheless. That dead silence on the airwaves said that a fine man with a great ministry felt incapable of relinquishing it if God asked.

We are called to two very different types of surrender. The last chapter of this book will deal with the most difficult challenge we face as Christians. Many of us are already feeling overwhelmed by the first eight chapters. But these are the easy ones. Adding an hour of prayer and Bible reading a day? Going to church? Loving others? Being sacrificial? Fasting? Learning how to listen, and opening our hearts to the potential to hear a serious call from God? Most who have journeyed this far have been able to do most of the requirements of the first seven chapters at some time in our lives, if only for a season, or we have done many parts almost all of the time. Jesus calls us to take the same posture as the disciples. He calls us to be prepared to turn our backs on jobs, possessions, friends, and family . . . and follow Him.

Are we prepared to do that? I have never discussed this with anyone who has even considered it. Friends with lots of possessions or almost nothing. Does not matter. Young or old. Plenty of close family or no family at all. It is not part of our Christian thinking to consider walking away from our comfy lives.

In case you are still reading, take the test. If you had a clear calling from God right now to walk away from your career, your wife and kids, your home and all other possessions in order to go serve Him in the worst rat hole you can think of, dealing with filth and disease, death and torment, would you go? What if you were called to start a political effort on a national basis to overcome the holocaust of abortion, including marches, picketing, even jail? Make it easier: just give up all your current possessions, including future earnings from pensions and Social Security, and give them to a cause.

How about the twelve disciples? What about Abraham? They did not know what they were being called to do. A controversial young rabbi tapped each of the twelve disciples on the shoulder and said, "Follow me." No, don't even tell your family goodbye or make arrangements for your being gone. Just "Follow me." God spoke to Abraham and told him to go over to a place unknown and start over.

The act of surrendering to a call always starts with God. The most common calling in our Christian walk is when God *calls* someone into the ministry or to a specific task. It is notable that such calls usually come during a time when the heart is more open, such as during a service, a retreat, a fast, or a revival of some kind.

In groups, in focused gatherings, the spiritual is mixed with the emotional and even the pressure of the crowd. The actions and expectations of the group put pressure on individuals. People who have been sitting on the fence may be looking for a boost. Because of the mixture of elements in place, there are false conversions, false rededications, and false decisions. But, because the hearts of some were truly open at that moment, there are also sincere decisions.

The openness that develops in these moments is very crucial to someone's ability to surrender to the call.

It is possible to hear a call from Jesus and then make a

true and sincere decision to follow Jesus during an *organized* meeting. I would encourage anyone to use those moments to become open and responsive to any leading.

It is also possible to make yourself available to God by a clear, careful, and conscious process. Just as some come to Jesus after careful consideration, and counting the cost, I believe that some of us simply offer ourselves to Him in surrender. We understand that we may later be called to do His work. We accept that the call may take us far outside of our comfort zone.

How does that happen? For me, it took a combination of a strong walk, a strong desire to serve, and getting past my fear, lack of faith, and unbelief. Do I have a strong walk? Mine is probably no stronger than yours. Do I desire to serve? Maybe really strong! Can I easily overcome my fear, unbelief and lack of faith?

I have addressed the two times that I surrendered in earlier chapters, so there is no good reason to go over the same ground. But I will say again that I knew that surrender to his will would ultimately require a decision to do his will. I don't take any of Jesus's words or deeds lightly, and it is obvious that He and the Father are looking for complete and utter surrender. My personal life verse became Isaiah 6:8. Let's put it up again.

Then I heard the voice of the Lord saying, "Whom shall I send? And who will go for us?" And I said, "Here am I. Send me!"

When I heard these words, I was thinking that Christ might "send me" to a bigger, better radio show, another book, or some other glamorous opportunity. I counted the cost, and I still count the cost before surrendering. What exactly will I be required to give up? What might I face?

Why are those questions important to me? Because I don't trust God. He might want me to go somewhere that I will hate. I might miss my friends and family. I might get hurt or be deprived of Western conveniences like medicine. I certainly am unlikely to have sunny days at 70 degrees with a 6 mph breeze, weather conditions that are almost guaranteed at my house in Los Angeles most of the year.

I don't believe God's words that He won't forsake me, or that everything will be fine for those who love Him. At least I don't believe them enough to surrender. What about you?

Here is my theory. **Our Christian walk is always about how much we trust and believe, and whether we trust God enough to put aside our fear.** Each stage of our maturing in Christ depends on our ability to repent of our unbelief, or pride, and our idols, and move to the next stage. This is true from our first profession of faith. It is true when we start each new discipline. It is true when we become aware of the depths of our sin and mindful of our need to be continually repenting. It is true when we become willing to be completely dependent on and open with God—intimate with Him.

Then we must repent of our unbelief again if we are to fully surrender to a calling. As I write this I have been on the verge of surrender again for five months. There is a short, but important list of reasons why I'm not ready. Does that sound like you when you were not quite ready to give the whole 10% tithe, or not quite ready to have a daily time with God? Does that also sound like you when you realized that you should never assert your rights with your spouse? Not quite ready? Don't believe and trust enough? Are you too fearful?

What surrender really means!

If you surrender to the prosecuting attorney because you have been charged with a crime, you walk away from everything by the force of the law. If you are on a battlefield and raise the white flag, you are surrendered to whatever your new masters have planned. Our God is the law, and Jesus is our Master. *Ironically, we have no more control over our lives when we*

God Called

choose not to surrender than if we do surrender. It just feels as if we do. God's promise is that we will experience great gain from surrender and great loss if we remain tied to the things of this world. He is either Lord of our lives, or He isn't. I believe that any mature Christian must always be on the verge of surrender. Maybe the dial is set on 7 out of 10 one day or year, and another time it is at 8 or 9. If not, we sing the song in vain, we pray the prayer in vain, and we tell others the good news in vain. Unlike us, God is not surprised that we need the help of the Holy Spirit to climb over the last hump on this leg of the journey. Give Him half a chance, and he will provide the courage and faith that you need to surrender fully to God's call on your life. Pray Isaiah 6:8 and see what God has in store.

Chapter 10—Be Holy

"There appeared unto them cloven tongues like as of fire."—*Acts ii. 3.*

Pentecost

I should be a great bowler, but I really stink at it. My Dad's family has amazing bowlers. At least two of my uncles had 300 games and my Poppy was ranked nationally. I bowled a lot. Had my own ball and my own shoes. I have never had a 200 game and during my league years averaged around 135. In case you don't know much about bowling, that is not a good score.

On the other hand, I am a very good hitter in baseball. I won't bore you with the details; just take my word for it. Why the difference?

When I bowl, I keep a set of rules in my head. I think about each one before delivering the ball. Hold your hand this way, start at this spot, take just three steps and end up on that spot, then deliver the ball with a certain speed, a kind of spin, and hit the mark on the alley. Don't forget to follow through. My brain is always at work. I can't get out of my own way. No matter how much I practice, the words are still in my head.

God Called

When I stand up to bat in baseball, there are no such rules. I learned to hit in the streets and at the park with no one telling me the rules. I don't need to put my feet any place special. My feet know what to do. I don't fiddle with my bat, or think about my form or my follow through. The ball comes, I swing, and the ball goes a long way.

In bowling, the rules control my game. In baseball the rules are etched on my heart by playing the game. When the bat connects perfectly there is a sensation of joy that is hard to explain. I never have that joy in bowling, even when the ball goes exactly where I desire.

Another example. If you play video games, you know that there is a point in any fast paced, level-based game where you can no longer think about your moves. You must step outside of yourself and trust your brain, muscle memory, and instincts to take over. If you fail to get outside of yourself, you will fail in the game.

Francis Chan touched my heart in his book, *Crazy Love*, when he pointed out that a surfer cannot fight the wave. To try is pure folly as the wave is massively more powerful than the surfer. The rider must go with the wave and let it carry him. Years of trial and error allow the surfer to trust the nature of waves and rely on what his body has learned so that he can simply let go.

I love being a parent, and now a Poppy. I have read many dozens of books on parenting. My folks had four children, and I was the oldest, so I observed parenting in action. I don't have a bunch of rules about my parenting. I feel no pressure to push my kids one way or the other regarding careers or hobbies. There is no sense that their successes and/or failures reflect on me. On the other hand, I feel profoundly responsible for the way I parent. I am confident that providing them with love, introducing them to Jesus, and training them in right living are my most important jobs in this life. It is this combination of being responsible, yet allowing for freedom, that Paul kept driving at in his letters to the churches.

On the other hand, I can take a hard look at my role as husband. In similar fashion I studied marriage in college, read at least 100 books on the subject from both secular and Christian authors, and I have been married my entire adult life. I saw my parent's 63-year marriage, so I had an outstanding model. Still, I suspect that I hold on too tight here. I don't trust my instincts as much, and I am careful rather than free.

I could easily laugh this off with an offhand comment about the complexity of women compared to hitting a baseball or catching a wave. But the plain truth is, in marriage it is harder for me to *let go* and allow God to take care of things.

HOLINESS THROUGH SURRENDERING EVERYTHING TO GOD

With that massively long introduction, I will discuss a part of the Christian life where we all struggle, where my thoughts on the subject are riding on my prayers that the Holy Spirit will guide me to offer something that is helpful: holiness.

In Ephesians 4, Paul says:

That, however, is not the way of life you learned when you heard about Christ and were taught in him in accordance with the truth that is in Jesus. You were taught, with regard to your former way of life, to put off your old self, which is being corrupted by its deceitful desires; to be made new in the attitude of your minds; and to put on the new self, created to be like God in true righteousness and holiness.

Therefore each of you must put off falsehood and speak truthfully to your neighbor, for we are all members of one body. "In your anger do not sin": Do not let the sun go down while you are still angry, and do not give the devil a foothold. Anyone who has been stealing must steal no longer, but must work, doing something useful with their own hands, that they may have something to share with those in need.

Do not let any unwholesome talk come out of your mouths, but only what is helpful for building others up according to their needs, that it may benefit those who listen. And do not grieve the Holy Spirit of God, with whom you were sealed for the day of redemption. Get rid of all bitterness, rage and anger, brawling and slander, along with every form of malice. Be kind and compassionate to one another, forgiving each other, just as in Christ God forgave you.

Ephesians 4:20-32 (Emphasis added)

I know that I fall massively short of this standard. Not just on Christmas and Easter. Not just on Sunday. Not just for a season. Every day. I thank Jesus for taking on my sin. We know that we are saints who sin, but that can't be an excuse or justification for our sin. Repenting is part of the response, and repentance includes turning from that sin. There is more. We must completely surrender our lives to God. We don't own anything. It is all on rent. We don't really control anything, no matter how hard we try. The wave, our kids and our spouses can't be controlled. We have already spoken the words of surrender when we make the decision to come to Christ.

So why don't we live here on earth as life is in heaven. You know the reasons. Lack of trust. Lack of faith. Unbelief. We don't trust God's control, and we try to control what we think we can control.

In one of my favorite books of the last 20 years, "Final Quest," author Rick Joyner describes a scene where his traveler comes upon a prison by the side of the road. There is a prisoner looking through the bars and bemoaning his predicament.

The traveler eventually walks around the other side of this small building to find that it is wide open in the back. The prisoner only need walk out. He feels safer in that prison than walking out and facing life. We are all in that place with regard to some aspect of our life. For me it is bowling, and struggling to give up my desire to fix things that are better left to God.

I humbly submit some ideas that may help you mature to the kind of submission that will move you along the path towards greater holiness, and thus provide you with total freedom.

Fear God

Did you fear your dad when you were growing up? Maybe your mom, too? When you were considering doing something *bad*, did you consider the cost if caught? Probably so. With your Heavenly Father, you are already caught when you first consider the sin. You are caught while committing it. And you are caught while covering it, making excuses for it, or lying to Him about it.

Moreover, because God is Holy, He cannot tolerate that sin, and must turn away from you while you are sinning. Though, as a Christian, you are forgiven for all sins past, present, and future, that does not mean that you can maintain fellowship with God while sinning, that He will bless you while you are in sin, or that consequences aren't built into your transgression, forgiven or not.

If you believe the Bible, then you must believe that God is to be feared. Moreover, while your salvation is assured, you still must face Jesus and give an accounting. Ultimately we will suffer gain or loss in heaven based on our decisions here on earth. Is it worth the consequences on earth or heaven to watch that porn, tell that joke, gossip about that person, or waste your time and treasure.

Deciding Every Day

If you or I determine to move on this path of being fully surrendered to God, there will be plenty of other forces enticing

God Called

us to turn away from this narrow road. There will be plenty of beings, both physical and spiritual, who will intentionally or unwittingly entice us to change course. Our fleshly, worldly instincts will generate itches that demand to be scratched.

Remembering and recommitting to our plan for Holy living at the beginning of the day seems only too obvious as a wise strategy to improve our chances of achieving victory.

Continual conversation

For years I struggled with the Bible verses that suggested we pray continuously. In meetings with mature believers, this turned out to be a common bit of confusion. I ultimately came to the conclusion that if the word of God is the foundation of our life, the Holy Spirit is going to bring it to mind as needed all throughout the day. We won't necessarily need to stop and ask for directions at every street corner.

Dallas Willard goes much further in his book, *Hearing God*. He suggests that we have a continuous conversation with God throughout the day, in much the same way we might with our spouse, a close co-worker, or a friend. The conversation might take the form of sharing thoughts, intentions, plans, or rehashing of recent decisions or actions to determine outcomes or improvements. This would go much beyond what I am pretty sure is our standard outgoing single prayer of "please heal Jimmy" and "thank you for blessing me in this or that way." As with any person who might share in that conversation, the Holy Spirit can listen intently, offer encouragement, provide comfort, or suggest alternatives.

If we are committed to full surrender, it is critical to be in touch with God throughout the day.

Immersion

My youngest son, Robert, played high school baseball for

a coach who hammered on the idea that baseball needed to be their *number one focus*. The team members were constantly reminded that they needed to be playing the game, thinking about the games, and watching others play the game. This approach recognizes that when we are immersed in an activity, it provides training to every part of our being, and keeps out distractions that might work against the goals.

In my personal walk, immersion is a key component of any success. As soon as I turn off the news, and the TV, and put aside secular entertainment, my life changes almost immediately. According to Christian pollster, George Barna, "Born-again Christians spend seven times as much time on entertainment as they do on spiritual activities."[5] Imagine what the percentages might be if you compared all forms of secular input with all types of Christian input. I imagine the percentage would be much higher.

Just imagine if your car radio and TV only played Christian material. Or what if you turned off your TV and spent the 3—5 hours per day you are probably spending now on sit-coms, cop shows, and other programming, and spent that time with Christian authors, speakers, preachers, community with other believers, and outreach. Think of the difference in what would be on your mind and affecting your thinking.

When was the last time you watched a TV show of any kind that had no characters on the show who were involved in blatant sexual sin. Try this: Watch any kid's sitcom and see how many times per minute somebody is lying about something in order to stay out of trouble, and with absolutely no thought of it being wrong, and no consequence.

Try immersing yourself for a period of time: 40 days, 90 days, a year. Once you have started the practice, you will find great joy in the experience, but you will also find that it helps you towards holiness. When I am immersed, I prefer to listen to Christian talk radio in the car. The impact of hearing one or two sermons per day is profound. I know others who prefer praise music, of which there is an almost unlimited selection in every genre.

At home, I generally turn to Christian books, both fiction and non-fiction, and turn off the TV completely. Of course there are numerous programs and movies available that are biblically sound. Some of my friends are enjoying audio books and podcasts.

There is also a wealth of sermons on YouTube on almost every verse in the Bible from multiple pastors. The Charles Spurgeon sermons on the Beatitudes mentioned above are so incredible that I have now spent almost 30 hours listening to them over and over.

Be careful, however, the world has a way of creeping back in, one half hour game show at a time. I feel sure that God intends for us to make time for relaxation and mindless activity that provides a time to refresh. However, the very use of the word *mindless* is problematic. Your mind is not turned off during these mindless times.

Have a mentor, be a mentor

Noted Pastor and past president of the Dallas Theological Seminary, Charles Swindoll, talks about the fact that his board of directors monitors his Christian walk. Periodically, they ask him a series of questions about his recent activities to see if he is off the path. The last question on the list is: "Did you just lie about any of our questions in your answers?"

Are you close enough to anyone, that you could reveal any sinful behavior you have engaged in? Is this person tough enough to ask you the hard questions and give you the hard answers?

Have you offered yourself as one who could be trusted to hear someone else's confession? Are you tough enough to speak

Godly wisdom to this person, even when it would be easier to help them with excuses?

Go about God's work

When Jesus tells two stories with the same basic plot, it is usually a good idea to pay notice. Therefore, it seems pretty clear that God will not be happy with people who have buried the talents God has loaned them for this earthly journey.

If you have heard God's call on your life, get busy with it. If you haven't yet heard anything specific or clear, get busy with some kind of work that utilizes your gifts. Please do not tell me you have no gifts. The Bible says in 1 Corinthians 12 that each person has at least one gift of the spirit. Most such statements arise from false modesty or low self-worth. God says you are valuable. Believe Him.

For a time I belonged to a church with a wonderful member whose ministry was to send birthday cards, anniversary cards, and other cards for births, condolences, and graduations. There was a hand written note in each card. All who received them cherished these notes. It sounds like a lowly, simple gift, but no gift is lowly in God's kingdom. You have a gift. Simply do the Lord's work, and you will have less time to stray from Holiness.

I am blessed you have traveled with me to the end of this journey. The deeper hope is that it is only the beginning of many journeys you will travel in answer to God's call on your life. Feel free to contact me at RandyKirk77@gmail.com. I would love to hear how this book helps you.

End Notes

1) Text and translation from http://www.bible-researcher.com/schmeling.html
2) Dallas Willard, *Hearing God* (Downers Grove, IL, Intervarsity Press, 2012)
3) The *International Children's Bible*, published by Thomas Nelson is available through most major booksellers
4) *The Answer: Authentic Faith for an Uncertain World* published by Thomas Nelson is available through most major booksellers
5) George Barna (Barna Group https://www.barna.org/barna-update/article/5-barna-update/180-americans-donate-billions-to-charity-but-giving-to-churches-has-declined#.UvhGvV4xs5A).

Recommended for Further Reading

Anderson, Neil, *The Bondage Breaker*, (Eugene, Harvest House Publishers, 1990)

Chan, Francis, *Crazy Love: Overwhelmed by a Relentless God*, (Colorado Springs, David C Cook, 2013

Colson, Chuck, with Vaughn, Ellen Santilli, *The Body: Being Light in the Darkness*, (Dallas, Word Publishing, 1992

Joyner, Rick, *Final Quest*, (Fort Mill, Morningstar Publications, 1996)

Keller, Timothy, Kings Cross, (London, Hodder & Stoughton, 2012)

Roberts, Richard Owen, *Repentance: The First Word of the Gospel*, (Wheaton, Crossway, 2002)

Spurgeon, Charles, Beatitudes sermons on YouTube, http://bit.ly/Beatitudes1

Photo Credits

Page

5 Courtesy of Pearl, www.lightstock.com, standard license
15 Graphic by Randy Kirk, hymn text in public domain
21 Photograph by Randy Kirk
23 Courtesy of Pete Unseth at Wikimedia Commons, image in the public domain
26 Courtesy of Pam Kirk
29 Courtesy of Library of Congress at http://www.loc.gov/blog/?p-140
34 Courtesy of Tom Nichols
36 Courtesy of Bill Stockwell
39 The Sermon on the Mount Carl Bloch, 1890, image is in public domain
44 Courtesy of www.dreamstime.com standard license
54 Courtesy of www.lightstock.com standard license
70 Photograph by Randy Kirk
72 Courtesy of Gstockstudio at www.dreamstime.co standard license
74 http://ibc.lynxeds.com/
87 Caravaggio 1598 This image is in public domain
93 Artist Desconocido This image is in public domain

www.ingramcontent.com/pod-product-compliance
Lightning Source LLC
Chambersburg PA
CBHW051953290426
44110CB00015B/2219